Slipping Through My Fingers

What Every Mother Feels.

What Every Daughter Will One Day Understand.

Aderonke "Ronnie" Izon

Third Act Society

Copyright

To every mother who stood at the edge of goodbye with a smile on her face and a prayer in her heart.

And to every daughter who will one day understand.

Table of Contents

Preface

This isn't just my story. It's yours too. We'll walk this road together.

The morning I stood barefoot on cold asphalt, chasing a garbage truck while calling my daughter's nickname into the dawn air, I realized I had become a stranger in my own life. For years, that Tuesday morning routine had belonged to our family - first her older brothers, then passed down to her. Now it was just me, clutching an empty trash bin as evidence of everything I'd lost.

My seventeen-year-old daughter had left for college, and I was completely unprepared for the silence that followed.

If you've ever stood in the hallway between who you were and who you are evolving into, this book is your companion.

While my words speak primarily to mothers navigating the identity shift, this journey extends to women across all seasons of life. If you're a younger mother with children still at home, these pages offer a glimpse of the road ahead and a gentle reminder to savor the present moments that seem endless but pass so quickly. If you're well beyond this threshold, you may find words for experiences you've lived but perhaps never fully articulated. And if you're standing right at the doorway of goodbye, know that the path ahead, though unmarked, is not unwalked.

You will not only read about my journey of letting go and rediscovery. You will reflect, release, and redefine your next act alongside me.

This is the power of shared stories. They remind us that even in our most solitary moments, we are never truly alone. The emotions that catch in your throat as you fold that last load of laundry before they leave, the questions that keep you awake when their bedroom is empty, the surprising joy you discover when you begin to reclaim yourself, these experiences connect us across differences, across generations, across life's varied pathways.

So wherever you stand on this journey, I invite you to turn these pages not just as a reader, but as a fellow traveler. The Third Act awaits us both.

Here's what I didn't know when I started this journey: according to recent reports from Fortune and Entrepreneur, I'm part of a 73 million woman demographic that controls $15 trillion in global wealth. We're the most economically powerful generation of women in human history, yet somehow we've been convinced our most valuable years are behind us when our children leave home.

The math doesn't add up.

We've reached our peak earning years, our highest investment potential, our maximum wealth-building decades. We finally have discretionary income to spend on our own dreams instead of everyone else's needs. Yet the culture treats us like we're disappearing just when we're gaining the confidence, connections, and capital to change everything.

Growing up Nigerian taught me that women gain power with age, not lose it. Mothers become matriarchs. Wisdom increases value. Experience commands respect. But, American culture had me believing I should gracefully step aside when my children no longer needed daily care, as if my only worth was measured by how much others needed me.

That collision between what my heritage taught me about women's value and what my adopted culture expected nearly broke me. Until I realized millions of women worldwide are caught in this same gap between cultural expectations and economic reality.

The woman who drove 206,000 miles in carpools wasn't just shuttling children to activities. She was developing project management skills, crisis resolution abilities, and the kind of patience that builds leaders. The mother who managed three children's schedules while working full time wasn't just surviving. She was mastering logistics that Fortune 500 companies pay consultants millions to figure out.

Those skills don't become obsolete when the children leave. They become available for new purposes.

This book exists because transformation keeps happening whether we participate or not. The question isn't whether you'll change after your children launch. The question is whether you'll change with intention or just let life happen to you.

I'm writing this ten years into my own Third Act, not from the mountaintop of having it all figured out, but from the ongoing work of becoming the woman I know I am called to be. Because here's what I've learned: transformation isn't a destination you reach. It's a path you walk. Not linear, not perfect, far from perfection because it doesn't exist, but worth every uncertain step.

> *"Fear ye not me? saith the Lord: will ye not tremble at my presence, which have placed the sand for the bound of the sea by a perpetual decree, that it cannot pass it: and though the waves thereof toss themselves, yet can they not prevail; though they roar, yet can they not pass over it?"— Jeremiah 5:22 (KJV)*

Let this be the stillness at the edge of every storm. A reminder that even the most roaring tides know where to stop.

Prologue

November 2014

I called her name before I remembered she was gone.

"Charlie!" I shouted up the stairs, the way I had every Tuesday morning for the past five years. "Trash truck!"

Silence that answered back hit me like a freight train. Not the defiant silence of a teenager pretending not to hear. Not the busy silence of someone getting ready. Just... nothing. Empty space where her voice should be, where her footsteps should be thundering down the stairs, where her complaints about Tuesday morning chores should be filling our house with the beautiful, ordinary noise of a life being lived.

She was three states away, building a future I'd taught her to want, living the independence I'd spent seventeen years preparing her for. And I was standing at the bottom of stairs she'd never run down again as a teenager, calling for someone who didn't need to answer the 'trash truck is here' call anymore. That's when I realized I hadn't just raised independent children. I'd erased myself in the process.

This isn't a story about empty nest syndrome. It's about what happens when you wake up and discover that the woman you used to be has vanished so completely that even you can't find her. When you've spent so many years being essential to everyone else that you've become invisible to yourself.

But buried underneath all that forgetting was a letter waiting to be written. A move across the country that would teach me about coming home. And a discovery that the third act of a woman's life isn't about what you've lost - it's about what you're brave enough to find.

Because somewhere between that empty staircase and the woman staring back from my mirror was a revolution waiting to happen. Not just for me, but for the 73 million women controlling $15 trillion in wealth stepping into this same threshold, wondering if they'll disappear completely or discover they were just getting started.

If you've ever looked in the mirror and wondered who's staring back, this story is for you.

"There are only two lasting bequests we can hope to give our children. One of these is roots, the other, wings."

— Johann Wolfgang von Goethe

Introduction

I became a mother at twenty-seven and forgot to remain a woman.

My daughter JoAnna, Charlie to me, left for college at seventeen. Not because she was running away, but because I'd raised her so well she was ready to fly before I was ready to let go.

For twenty-three years, I perfected the art of disappearing into other people's needs. Three children taught me to sense fevers from across the house, pack lunches that said "I love you" in peanut butter and jelly, and turn my body into a human shield against every disappointment the world might dare send their way.

I could negotiate with teachers, survive on four hours of sleep, and make Christmas magic happen on a grocery store budget. But ask me what I wanted for dinner when no one else had an opinion? I'd stand paralyzed in my own kitchen, a stranger to my own preferences.

This is the story of what happens when your greatest success as a mother feels like your greatest loss as a woman. When the child you spent seventeen years teaching to need you less finally doesn't need you at all. When you realize you've been training for a job that was always meant to end.

It's the story of standing barefoot on cold asphalt at dawn, chasing a garbage truck because you forgot that Tuesday morning trash duty was no longer ours, it was mine. Of crying in coffee shops while writing letters you never planned to share. Of discovering that letting go isn't a single moment of brave release, but a thousand small deaths that somehow birth you into a life you never knew you wanted.

But mostly, it's the story of what happens when you stop trying to hold on and start learning to bless forward, when you discover that your Third Act isn't an ending, but the beginning of the third act you never saw coming.

If you're reading this, chances are you know this ache. The sacred grief of raising children who no longer need raising. The beautiful terror of rediscovering who you are when no one is calling your name.

Your third act is waiting. Let's walk toward it together.

1

The Day My Purpose Walked Out the Door

"To every thing there is a season, and a time to every purpose under the heaven... A time to keep, and a time to cast away."— Ecclesiastes 3:1,6 (KJV)

***

We parent with our whole hearts because there is no other way. When they grow up, our hearts don't shrink back. We don't stop - truth is, we simply don't know how. We're not equipped. The nonexistent manual never said on page 15, "Independence is coming up around the bend."

Here's the brutal truth no one prepares you for: Every child who leaves takes a piece of your purpose with them. When your last child walks out the door, you realize - perhaps suddenly - you've been preparing yourself out of the most important job you'll ever love.

I remember standing in that college auditorium in 2015, surrounded by hundreds of nervous parents, when the professor asked us to raise our hands. First question: "How many of you are sending your firstborn to college?"

Several hands shot up around me. I didn't raise mine. I sat back, arms crossed, feeling an odd sense of superiority. Rookies, I thought.

This was my third rodeo. I'd done this twice before with the boys. I knew the drill. Pack, drive, unpack, hug, leave. Simple mathematics of parenting.

"And how many of you," he continued, scanning the room, "are sending your last child to college today? How many of you are about to become empty nesters?"

My hand shot up so fast it surprised even me. There was almost a pride in it - a graduation of my own. Look at me, a veteran, finishing my tour of duty. I've raised three children and I'm about to cross the finish line.

I had no idea I wasn't graduating from anything. I was being thrown into exile from the only job that ever mattered. I was being thrust into a foreign country without a map, without a language guide, without preparation.

The professor nodded at those of us with raised hands, and there was something in his eyes, a knowing, a gentle warning perhaps, that I completely missed.

"For those of you becoming empty nesters," he said, his voice softening, "this transition might hit differently than you expect. Even if you've done this before."

I barely registered his words. I was too busy feeling accomplished.

Then he shifted to his advice about communication. "Want your kid to call you? Easy. Write them a letter. Email them. Say, 'I was thinking of you and thought you may be out of cash, so I'm including $100.'"

He laughed. We laughed.

"They'll call. Fast."

And I laughed with the other parents. I nodded like I was okay with this transaction of love for communication. I played along with the charade of "this is fine."

But what I didn't know then, what I couldn't possibly have prepared for, was the weight that awaited me. The tension headaches that would come from holding back tears. The physical ache in my throat from swallowing goodbyes. The stunning silence that would fill every corner of my home like an unwelcome fog.

Nobody prepared me for the day my job would become obsolete.

The Cultural Tightrope

What made this transition, this power shift, even more complex was that I was navigating it with an African mother's heart in an American parenting reality.

Millions of women are navigating this same cultural collision. We're caught between traditions where respect flowed bottom-up, children to parents, where children had ears for listening rather than voices for questioning, and a culture that expects us to disappear when our children leave. This isn't personal confusion, it's systematic displacement that deserves recognition and response.

In the culture where I was raised, children don't just "leave home." They expand the home. They bring spouses and grandchildren back to the nest, creating layers of family that grow wider, not thinner. Mothers don't become irrelevant; they become matriarchs. The older you get, the more essential you become, not less.

But here I was, in a culture that celebrated independence as the ultimate parenting success story, while my African soul screamed that something fundamental was wrong with this picture.

I thought of my mother, still needed daily by extended family, still the center of decisions, still the keeper of wisdom that grows more valuable with time. And here I was, being congratulated for successfully making myself unnecessary.

The collision of these two worldviews - honor your elders versus set them free - was happening inside my chest every single day.

The Paradox of Choice

The irony wasn't lost on me. For seventeen years, I'd been training my daughter to make choices. Even as babies when they can't even recognize colors, we hold up two choices and ask in baby tones, "Which one? Left or right?" - as if they really have a choice.

I think of my daughter at eight months old, sitting in her high chair, me holding two different pureed foods in front of her. "Peas or sweet potatoes?" I'd ask as if she could comprehend the question. But she'd reach for one, her tiny hand grasping toward the orange mush instead of the green. I would celebrate this "choice" as if she'd just demonstrated remarkable decision-making skills.

We continue as they're growing. How many times have you asked a toddler what they want? We proudly hold up two choices of whatever. WE give them the choice. We've been giving them choices since time immemorial. We move from two choices to outright asking, "What do you want for dinner? What do you want to do?"

You can fill in the gap if you're being honest with yourself.

And just when they decide to take us up on the same offer they've heard all their lives, we suddenly cry foul! Because they didn't file an application requesting to make their own choices, choices we know we will not approve, even if they asked.

The Mathematics of Motherhood

You've packed the bins. You've prayed the prayers. You've triple-checked the emergency contacts. If you're anything like me, you even asked for welfare check phone numbers, the roommate's number they only met online. Maybe even their roommate's parents. Kindred spirits. Mothers of freshmen, just like you, trying to hold on to something familiar in the unknown.

You may have exchanged group texts, silent promises to check in on each other's kids. You may even have the perfectly painted smiley band leader's number. Just in case. Because "just in case" is where our minds live.

But releasing a child? That's an act of surrender that nobody prepares you for.

By the time the professor was done talking, the kids were already busy living. Mine was off to sports or band, probably both. And there I was, standing with my arms halfway open and my heart already folding in on itself, crumpling like paper in a fist.

I barely got a hug in.

I remember the band leader, standing a few feet away like a marshal guarding the border between childhood and adulthood. She wore that smile, the one that says "We've got them now" while gently ushering you out of the picture with the same hands that just took your last check.

I hugged longer than I should have. I felt her shoulders tighten, the silent signal.

"Mom..." she whispered.

That one word held four meanings: Let go. You're smothering me. You're embarrassing me. Please, not here.

So I did. I let go. My arms. My breath. My everything.

And that was the moment I understood what the day your purpose walks out the door really meant.

It wasn't just a poetic metaphor. It was literal.

That Drive Home Shifted Something Fundamental

I remember standing in her dorm room, surrounded by the trappings of her new life, the extra-long twin sheets we'd argued over at the big box store ("Mom, I don't need the 800 thread count, the basic ones are fine"), the mini-fridge humming in the corner, the command hooks waiting to hold memories she hadn't made yet. Everything was in its place. Except my heart.

My heart was still caught somewhere between her childhood bedroom and this sterile box where strangers would now know her morning voice, her late-night habits, her unguarded moments that once belonged only to home.

I wanted to tell her roommate everything: "She sleeps with one foot outside the covers, always has. She laughs in her sleep sometimes. She's grumpy before her first sip of tea. She needs someone to remind her to eat when she's stressed."

But I bit my tongue, knowing these intimate details of motherhood were no longer mine to share. They were hers to reveal or conceal in her own time, in her own way.

Driving home became my education in grief. I'd driven her from Maryland to Elon, North Carolina. We'd had fun on the way up, singing to her playlist, stopping for snacks, talking about roommates and classes and all the possibilities ahead. But driving back alone? That was a different journey entirely.

The highway stretched before me, the same road I'd traveled just hours before, but now it felt entirely unfamiliar. The passenger seat beside me, her seat, was empty except for her forgotten sweatshirt, which I couldn't bring myself to move. I kept glancing over, the muscle memory of checking on her so ingrained that my neck turned without my permission.

The silence in the car was deafening. No music. No chatter about classes or friends. No complaints about my driving or requests to stop for snacks. Just the hum of tires on asphalt and the occasional ping of my phone that made my heart leap, hoping it was her, already missing me as much as I missed her.

You walk by their room and wonder, "Where did the time go?" You find their favorite snack in the pantry or the drink you'd stashed away hoping to surprise them. You blink back tears because they're not around to argue about why that brand is better than the one you bought.

I remember finding a half-eaten package of her favorite cookies tucked behind the cereal boxes months after she'd left. My first instinct was irritation, how many times had I reminded her not to leave open packages? Then came the wave of recognition: she wasn't here to remind anymore. The slightly stale cookies became a treasure, evidence of her presence, proof that she had been here, in this kitchen, in this life.

I remember one day, not long after Jason, my middle child left, he said to me: "Mom, you're so worried about us making mistakes. You hover and forget that we need to make our own mistakes to learn and grow." That hit me in the chest like a sermon. He wasn't being unkind. He was being truthful. And brave. We raise them to fly, but we thought we'd always be allowed to hover.

The Invisible Shift

The invisible shift. The slow fade. The letting go that starts long before you ever say goodbye.

I felt it first when Jason was about thirteen. He had always been my shadow, following me from room to room, telling me about his day, his thoughts, his dreams. On nights when I'd run late from work, he'd camp out on the couch waiting for me, calling to make sure I was okay and greeting me at the door with his playful 'Young lady, you're late!' - this sweet boy who worried about his mother like a protective older brother. And then one afternoon, I knocked on his bedroom door to call him for dinner, and he answered with a distracted, 'Yeah, I'll be down in a minute.' When he finally appeared at the table, he was present in body but absent in spirit, his mind elsewhere, his usual chatter replaced by monosyllabic responses..

I remember thinking, "Is this it? Is this how it begins?" This gradual distancing, this pulling away. No one had warned me it would start so soon, so subtly. No one had told me how it would feel like a small death. This ordinary moment of a teenage boy more interested in his friends' texts than his mother's questions.

There's an ache that lives beneath the surface. It's not loud. It doesn't shout. But it's there, like a low hum in your bones. You grieve the routines. The conversations. The chaos. The knowing where they are, even when it drove you crazy. And you feel silly sometimes. Ashamed to cry over something that's supposed to be beautiful. Natural. Expected. But here's what I've learned: Grief and gratitude are not opposites. They're companions. You can be grateful they're thriving, and still mourn the woman you were when they needed you every day.

I didn't jump into reinvention. I didn't grab a new hobby or book a solo trip. I sat. I wept. I wandered my own house like a stranger in a place I once ruled. I kept her sweatshirt close for three days. I cried in the grocery store. I avoided her favorite aisle. I counted the hours till her text came in.

And even then, it was short. "I'm good."

I wasn't. But I couldn't say that. Because mothers are supposed to be strong.

I remember a dad I met at that freshman orientation. He wasn't saying much, just quietly nodding along as the other parents shared packing tips and teary stories. But when someone asked how he was doing, he said softly, "I know she's ready. But I'm not. That's my baby girl." And we all felt it, the deep ache, not loud but loud enough to hollow out your chest.

His honesty was a gift. A permission slip for the rest of us to admit that while drop-off day is celebrated as a milestone of successful parenting, it's also a quiet funeral for a season ended too soon.

I spent months after the first drop-off living for the next holiday, the next break, the next chance to have my daughter back home. I marked the calendar, counted the days, planned menus for her return. I lived in anticipation. Always looking ahead. Never fully present in my own life.

Until one day, I realized I was missing my own. I was so focused on her next visit home that I was skipping through the pages of my own story.

That day, I decided to stop waiting and start living. To find joy not just in her return, but in the space her absence created. To explore not just what motherhood meant now, but what womanhood meant again.

Disguised Ending

My friend Jane described it as "phantom limb syndrome", this urge to parent a child who is no longer present to be parented. The reflexive reaching for a connection that has shifted form. The muscle memory of a role that has evolved.

"I still wake up at 6:30 a.m.," she told me, "even though there's no one to drive to school. I still cook too much pasta, even though there's only two of us eating now. I still listen for the front door opening at curfew time, even though there's no curfew to enforce."

I understood. These weren't just habits; they were expressions of love that had nowhere to go. The energy of motherhood, still flowing but redirected. But even in the breaking, there's a whisper: This is not the end of your story. You're still in the middle. You're allowed to ache. You're allowed to pause. You're allowed to say, "This hurts." Because healing doesn't begin with reinvention. It begins with honesty.

So, sit here as long as you need. In the grief. In the missing. In the mess.

This is where transformation begins, not in rushing past the pain, but in allowing it to reshape you. Not in pretending strength, but in finding it within the vulnerability. Not in having all the answers, but in living the questions.

You are not just a mother releasing a child. You are a woman evolving. And this evolution, painful as it is, is creating something beautiful, if you have the courage to see it through.

The truth about the day your purpose walks out the door: You're not just releasing a child into the world. You're releasing yourself into your next chapter. And that launch into your Third Act? It's the one that becomes your real beginning.

But first, I had to recognize the stranger in my mirror.

2

The Woman in the Mirror: Rediscovering Your Essential Self

"She is clothed with strength and dignity; she can laugh at the days to come."— Proverbs 31:25 (KJV)

***

I didn't recognize the woman staring back at me. She stood there in my bathroom mirror. Tired eyes. Shoulders carrying invisible weight. A smile that had forgotten how to reach her eyes. For a moment, I thought someone else had wandered into my reflection. Then the devastating realization hit: This stranger was me.

Twenty-three years of motherhood had sculpted my days, my thoughts, my very identity around three human beings who no longer needed me to manage their lives. And now, with their bedrooms empty and my calendar suddenly bare, I had no idea who I was beyond "Mom."

The mirror reflected back a question I wasn't prepared to answer: Who am I now? But to understand how I'd become unrecognizable to myself, you need to understand who that woman in the mirror used to be.

Her name was "Izon's Mom" - or "Mama Jeffrey" in Nigerian culture, where women are often called by their first child's name. And for over two decades, that was the only name that mattered. Society had taught me that this erasure was noble. That the complete disappearance of my own identity was proof of good mothering. But standing in that mirror, I began to question whether losing yourself was really necessary to love someone else well.

The Odometer of a Life Lived for Others

I put 206,000 miles on my brand-new Toyota Highlander driving them around. Let me say that again: 206,000 miles. That's eight trips around the entire Earth. That's driving from New York to Los Angeles 74 times. That's nearly a quarter of a million miles of my life measured in carpools, practices, games, tournaments, and the endless geography of other people's dreams.

From little league all the way to college football, basketball, choir, band, hockey, rugby, even ice hockey. Countless team mom roles. I still have my jersey emblazoned with "Izon's Mom" that I refuse to part with, as if it's a badge of honor from a war only mothers understand. But those weren't just miles. They were the gradual erasure of everything I used to be, one mile marker at a time.

Every exit on I-95 was another piece of myself I left behind. Every stadium parking lot was another place where I existed only in relation to someone else's development. I started to wonder: How many other women were driving similar routes, losing themselves mile by mile? How many other mothers were measuring their lives by odometers instead of their own achievements? It felt too systematic to be just coincidence.

The devastating mathematics of motherhood: We erase ourselves, one mile marker at a time. The odometer became the official record of how far I'd traveled from who I used to be.

All those miles were only possible because of the village that caught us when I couldn't be everywhere at once. Steve and Laurie, who I'd met at a salsa dance class back when I still did things for myself, stepped in during the early marital separation years. Laurie would pick up sick children from school when my job in DC made it impossible to leave.

Gene and Amy, our nextdoor neighbors in that first townhouse I bought in Odenton right after the separation, fed my boys dinner more nights than I can count when traffic or work kept me running late. Gene would offer to let the boys sleep at his house if I was going to be seriously delayed, or he'd camp out on the couch at mine to watch them.

The football coaches at Bowie Boys and Girls Club, Coach Pat, Coach Jim, Coach Franie, Coach Smitty and so many more, were more than coaches, they were pillars who understood family dynamics without judgment and filled gaps I didn't even realize existed. Without this constellation of people who chose to care about my children's well-being, those miles would have been impossible to drive.

Single motherhood taught me that it really does take a village, and I was blessed to find mine just when I needed them most. I drove from Bowie to Ocean City for so many little league Super Bowls I stopped counting. Highway 50 became as familiar as my own driveway. I've driven from Bowie, Maryland to College Hill in Providence, Rhode Island, to Morgantown, West Virginia, to Elon, North Carolina. The only drive I couldn't make was to Los Angeles when Charlie transferred to USC. Every mile was a pilgrimage to the altar of their growth, while mine slowly disappeared in the rearview mirror.

The Day My Identity Got Pulled Over

But there's one trip I'll never forget, the day my maternal devotion quite literally spilled onto the highway, and I got a front-row seat to just how completely I'd disappeared into my role.

Picture this: Me, flying down I-97 toward Virginia Beach at speeds that would make a NASCAR driver nervous. My faithful Highlander loaded to the brim with football gear. We were late, again, because someone couldn't find their cleats and someone else forgot their water bottle. I was doing that special mother-math where you calculate exactly how fast you need to drive to make up for every delay that wasn't your fault.

Red and blue lights in my rearview mirror.

I pulled over, heart pounding, and reached for my purse to get my license and registration. That's when the adrenaline fog cleared and I realized: we had left my handbag at home in our rush to be one of the first families to arrive in Virginia Beach.

The officer approached, all business and authority. "License and registration, ma'am."

I explained our predicament. No purse. No ID. Just a car full of football equipment and a mother who had completely lost her mind somewhere between the front door and the highway. He looked skeptical until I asked, "Can I check the trunk?"

I popped the hatch, and there it was: my entire identity spilling out in a rainbow of polyester and plastic. Jerseys with my children's names. Equipment bags labeled with our last name. Team schedules with my phone number listed as "Team Mom." Water bottles, first aid supplies, extra cleats in multiple sizes. Everything that proved I existed, but only in relation to someone else's dreams.

The officer looked at the mobile command center that was my car and softened. "You're really Team Mom, aren't you?"

"More than I'm anything else," I said, and for the first time, that admission felt like confession instead of pride.

He let me go with a warning and this advice: "Maybe get yourself an ID that has your name on it, not just theirs."

I drove the rest of the way to Virginia Beach understanding that I'd become so absorbed in their identities that I'd literally forgotten my own existed.

For two decades, I perfected the art of multiplication by division. I multiplied their happiness by dividing my attention. I expanded their opportunities by shrinking my own world. I celebrated their achievements while my accomplishments became footnotes in their stories.

This is the mathematics of motherhood. We multiply ourselves across their needs while dividing our own identity into ever-smaller fractions. We become experts in their preferences while forgetting our own. We memorize their dreams while letting ours fade to whispers. We build their confidence while ours quietly crumbles under the weight of constant self-sacrifice.

The thing about little league football is that it turns ordinary mothers into gladiators. I stand on the sidelines like a general surveying battlefields, analyzing plays we barely understand, cheering for strategies that exist mostly in my hopeful imaginations.

I was that mother. The one parents learned to position themselves strategically around when any of my boys touched the ball. Jason (JD as he was called at that time because another Jason was on the team), Jeffrey, and my nephew Richard, all running backs, all capable of turning me into a woman I didn't recognize the moment the coach called their number.

The particular Saturday that became family legend happened during Jason's best season. He was about ten or so, naturally athletic and fast as lightning, with that instinct for finding holes in the defense that can't be taught, only born. The weather was perfect, that crisp October air that makes football feel like the most important thing in the world.

The opposing team had been talking trash all morning, the kind of pre-game drama that turns little league football into serious business. Their coach kept shouting "shut down number 20" - that was my JD - and I was taking it personally.

When the play developed, everything unfolded exactly as Coach had drawn it up on his little whiteboard. Handoff to JD, hole opening left, my son cutting right with moves that made me want to call college scouts immediately. The crowd noise faded to a whisper as I watched him accelerate past the first defender, then the second, carrying the ball and every hope I'd ever invested in his confidence.

That's when I completely lost my mind.

I took off running parallel to the field, screaming like a banshee, which probably violated several county noise ordinances. "Go, JD! Go, go, go! Nobody can catch you!"

I was so focused on JD's progress, so caught up in the pure joy of watching my child succeed, that I completely forgot about the sweet woman filming beside me. She'd positioned herself carefully to capture her own son's big moment, camcorder steady, probably getting perfect footage of what should have been a routine play. JD cut right. I cut right. Physics took over.

Down went all three of us - me, her, and the camcorder that had been dutifully recording until it became part of our spectacular collision. For a moment, nobody moved. The play continued down the field while we sorted out limbs and dignity in a tangle that was equal parts embarrassing and absolutely hilarious.

"Oh my God, I'm so sorry!" I gasped, helping her to her feet while frantically checking her camera for damage. "I got carried away. Is your camcorder okay? Please tell me it's not broken."

She was laughing, thank God, the kind of full-body laughter that only comes when something is simultaneously mortifying and hilarious. "Ms. Izon," she said, brushing grass off her jeans, "if my son had made that run, I'd have done the same thing."

JD scored, by the way. Touchdown. But nobody was talking about his athletic achievement afterward. We became the story of the day, the cautionary tale parents would reference for years whenever someone got too enthusiastic on the sidelines. "Remember when Izon's mom took out the camcorder lady?" became shorthand for football parent intensity gone completely wrong.

The woman's footage survived, and she sent me a copy later. You can hear the exact moment when maternal pride overrode common sense. My voice getting louder and more animated until the screen goes sideways and all you hear is laughter.

But here's what that collision taught me about the mathematics of motherhood: love makes us do irrational things.

I can tell you every song that ever made my children happy, but I can't remember the last song that moved me to dance when no one was watching. For Jason, it was 'Sunday Best' by Surfaces: *'Feeling good, like I should, went and took a walk around the neighborhood, feeling blessed, never stressed, got that sunshine on my Sunday best.'* I can sing every word of that song. I know it lifted his mood when he was down.

I know every friend they've ever had. Every teacher they've struggled with. Every goal they've worked toward. But I couldn't tell you what I wanted for my own future beyond their happiness. Success in motherhood is measured by how well you eliminate your own necessity. Every milestone they reached, first steps, first day of school, first time driving alone, was them needing me a little bit less. I celebrated their independence while secretly mourning my own obsolescence.

The Gradual Disappearing Act

Losing yourself in motherhood doesn't happen overnight. It's a slow assassination of self, so gradual you don't notice until you're staring at a stranger in the mirror.

It starts with small compromises that feel like love. You postpone the book you wanted to read because they need help with homework. You skip the exercise class because they have practice. You decline dinner with friends because it's family night. Each choice feels right, feels necessary, feels like what a good mother does.

But slowly, your world shrinks to the size of their needs. Your calendar becomes their calendar. Your interests become their interests. Your dreams get filed under "someday when I have time." Your vocabulary shifts: "We have practice today" instead of "They have practice." "We made the team" instead of "They made the team." The lines blur until you can't tell where they end and you begin.

You became an expert in someone else's life while growing distant from your own. You memorized their preferences but forgot yours. You championed their dreams while yours collected dust. You solved their problems while your own questions went unanswered. You invested in their future while putting your own on indefinite hold.

The identity I'd built over two decades was so complete, so consuming, that when they no longer needed it daily, I didn't know what was left. The woman who used to have opinions about movies, who used to read novels for pleasure, who used to have dreams that had nothing to do with anyone else's future, where had she gone?

Standing in those mirrors, I realized she hadn't disappeared. She'd been buried. Buried under miles of football and band practice. Buried under years of putting everyone else's needs before her own. Buried under the weight of being indispensable to people who were now learning to live without her daily presence.

The first clue in the archaeological dig for my buried self came when I was cleaning out my daughter's closet and found a box of my old sketches from before the children were born. I sat on the floor and cried, not because I mourned my daughter leaving, but because I suddenly remembered this part of myself that had been packed away like those drawings. This woman who saw beauty and had to capture it. This woman who created things just because they needed to exist.

Another clue: The morning I woke up and didn't immediately think about what my children needed from me that day. Instead, for the first time in twenty years, I asked myself: "What do I want to do today?" The question felt foreign, almost transgressive.

What did I want? I'd been so focused on everyone else's wants and needs that my own desires had become uncharted territory.

The identity shift revelation is not just that your children are gone. It's that the version of yourself you've been for the last two decades suddenly has no clear mission. No daily purpose. No clear identity.

You spent years making yourself indispensable to people who were supposed to become independent. You measured your success by how well you anticipated their needs, solved their problems, facilitated their dreams. And then one day, they don't need you to do any of those things anymore. The woman you became in service to their development suddenly has no one to serve but herself. And if you're like me, you realize you've forgotten how to be your own priority.

The Three Acts of a Woman's Life

It was during one of those sleepless nights, staring at the ceiling of my empty house, that the framework came to me. Not in a blinding revelation, but in the quiet way truth settles when you finally stop running from it. Like a play where you are both the protagonist and, eventually, the director. And most women get stuck thinking Act Two is the final curtain.

Act One: The Sapling Years

I thought about my early twenties, that season of pure possibility when everything felt possible and nothing felt permanent. Fresh out of college, newly married, discovering what it meant to be American by choice rather than birth. Those were the years when I bent easily in strong winds, sometimes breaking, but always growing.

In Act One, we establish our roots through education, early relationships, career beginnings. We reach toward the sun of our own potential, absorbing everything we can about who we might become. We are green, flexible, eager to prove ourselves worthy of the space we occupy.

I remembered the young woman I was then, bold enough to move from Nigeria to America for school, confident enough to believe I could build a life from scratch, naive enough to think the hardest parts were behind me once I figured out the basics of survival.

That woman had opinions about everything. She had dreams that belonged to no one but herself. She stayed up late reading novels just because they moved her. She danced in her apartment to music that had nothing to do with anyone else's taste.

Where had she gone?

Act Two: The Mighty Oak

Then came the season I knew best. The decades when I became the shelter for others. My roots went deeper. My trunk grew wider. I stood firm against storms, measuring my success by how well those in my shade could thrive. This is the season when we become everything to everyone except ourselves.

Act Two was where I'd lived for over two decades. The years of being a mother, caregiver, protector, provider. The season when my worth was determined by how completely I could anticipate and meet the needs of others. When my calendar belonged to sport schedules and parent-teacher conferences. When my body existed to nurture, my mind to solve other people's problems, my heart to hold other people's dreams.

In Act Two, we measure our success by the thriving off those in our shade.

I'd been magnificent in Act Two. I'd raised three humans who were now confidently navigating the world. I'd built careers while building family meals. I'd managed crises with grace and celebrated victories with pure joy. I'd been the oak tree my family could depend on, standing strong through every storm that threatened their growth.

But somewhere in all that standing strong, I'd forgotten that trees don't stop growing just because they provide shelter. I'd confused being essential with being invisible.

Act Three: The Fullest Glory

And now? Now I was standing at the threshold of something I'd never imagined: the season when the oak tree reaches its fullest expression. Not the beginning of the end, but the most expansive, expressive, and potentially powerful season of all.

The mirror showed me a woman who had weathered decades of seasons, who had wisdom earned through storms survived and growth sustained. My canopy could spread wider than ever. My roots reached depths I couldn't have imagined in my sapling days. I could bear fruit not just for my immediate family but for widening circles of community.

And this was the revelation that shifted my perspective completely: I had decades of growth still ahead.

The recognition came gradually, like dawn breaking over a familiar landscape that looks completely different in new light. The calling doesn't come from outside yourself, but from within, from the parts of you that have been waiting patiently to be remembered.

I still keep my sons' leather jackets from one little league football championship in pristine condition, wrapped in tissue paper like a museum artifact. I have boxes of their trophies that became my most prized possessions. Not my own achievements - I have no idea where my college diplomas are – only their achievements. Evidence of what was my life. Those boxes have moved with me from Maryland to Texas, and back to Maryland. Through divorce. Through heartbreak. Through every major life transition.

Those trophies aren't just sports awards. They're the physical proof that I existed. That I mattered. That I was somebody important to somebody. They're tiny monuments to the complete reorganization of a life around other people's dreams.

I heard it first while unpacking their trophies in my Houston apartment. As I carefully arranged plastic figurines that celebrated other people's victories, a voice so faint I almost missed it: "Where are your trophies? What victories belong to you alone?"

The question stopped me cold. For twenty-three years, my victories had been measured in their achievements. Their good grades, their team wins, their college acceptances, their career successes. But what had I achieved that was mine alone?

It started with small moments of awareness after that. Catching myself in the grocery store buying food I didn't particularly like out of habit. Realizing I'd been watching television shows chosen for family harmony rather than my own interest. Noticing that my closet was full of clothes chosen for practicality rather than joy.

The voice came again during quiet moments: "Remember when you loved the sound of rain?" I did. I used to love listening to rain beating down on rooftops during summer storms, mesmerized by the power and beauty of nature unleashed. When had I stopped making time for wonder?

"Remember when you used to write?" Stories, thoughts, observations that mattered to no one but me. When was the last time I'd put pen to paper for my own pleasure?

"Remember when you had opinions about books that weren't on their reading lists?" Yes. I used to devour audiobooks by David Baldacci, Lee Child, James Patterson, losing myself in stories that had nothing to do with homework help or summer reading requirements. It used to drive Charlie crazy how I would slow down once we entered our neighborhood, stretching out those final minutes of listening time. I would drive past the house just to keep listening, circling the block because I couldn't bear to pause the story, while she rolled her eyes in the passenger seat, eager to get home.

"Remember when you dreamed of traveling?" I had dreamed of seeing the world, not just driving to other people's destinations. Not another 206,000 miles of carpools and tournaments, but passport stamps and boarding passes with my name alone.

That whisper grew louder: "Remember when you believed you had something unique to offer?" I had believed that. Before the believing got buried under decades of believing in everyone else.

These whispers weren't just about specific activities or dreams deferred. They were invitations back to myself. Back to the woman who existed before motherhood became my primary identity. Before my days were measured by other people's needs. Before my success was determined by how completely I could disappear into someone else's growth.

But here's what I discovered: The woman staring back at me wasn't broken. She wasn't lost. She was a veteran of the most important campaign of her life, and now she was being called to reclaim her authority in a new mission. One that required all the skills she'd developed, but directed toward a different target.

Herself.

The years of driving hadn't been wasted. They'd been training. Training in logistics, in crisis management, in seeing the best in others even when they couldn't see it themselves. Every team mom role had taught me about leadership. Every carpool had been a masterclass in efficiency. Every tournament had built resilience I didn't know I possessed.

And now? Now I was ready to use those skills to plan something for myself. Something that had nothing to do with anyone else's schedule or needs or dreams. The voice was calling me home to myself. And for the first time in decades, I was ready to answer.

The travel dreams? They weren't just dreams anymore. They were plans. Boarding passes. Passport stamps. Evidence that the woman who spent years driving everyone else to their destinations had finally found her own.

As the Three Acts framework crystallized in my mind, something else became clear: **This wasn't just my story. This was THE story.**

The women I was meeting, Sarah from the grocery store. Maria, whose kids had scattered. Janet navigating divorce and identity shift simultaneously. We were all standing at the same threshold. We were all women who'd mastered Act Two and had no idea what Act Three was supposed to look like.

The framework wasn't just helping me make sense of my own transition. It was giving language to something millions of women were experiencing without words for it.

Sitting in coffee shops, I'd watch women light up when I described the Three Acts. "Yes!" they'd say. "That's exactly what this feels like! I've been the oak tree for so long, I forgot I was still supposed to be growing!"

"I know who I was in Act One," Sarah said during one of our Tuesday morning gatherings. "And I was phenomenal in Act Two. But Act Three feels like this terrifying blank space where nobody tells you what you're supposed to do next."

"Because nobody knows," Maria added. "We're the first generation of women raised to believe we could be anything, who then spent decades being mothers, and now we're supposed to figure out what 'anything' means again."

The voice wasn't just calling me home to myself. It was calling me to help other women find their way home too.

Recognition, Release, Reclamation, Renewal

The mirror became a daily practice in transformation.

Recognition: Looking honestly at who I'd become and who I'd forgotten. Acknowledging both the woman who'd loved so completely she had disappeared and the woman who was ready to emerge.

Release: Letting go of the roles that no longer fit, the expectations that no longer served, the patterns that no longer brought life. Not abandoning my identity as a mother, but expanding beyond it.

Reclamation: Purposefully taking back my right to have preferences, needs, and dreams. Remembering what brought me joy before joy became something I facilitated for others.

Renewal: Stepping into Act Three with intention, understanding that this wasn't about starting over but about moving forward with everything I'd gained.

The woman in the mirror wasn't broken or lost. She was ready.

Months into my journey of rediscovery, the woman in the mirror started looking familiar again. Not because I'd reverted to who I was before motherhood, but because I'd done the sacred work of integration.

I could see the woman I'd been in Act One. Bold, curious, and willing to risk everything for growth. I could honor the woman I'd been in Act Two. Patient, nurturing, and fierce in her protection of others. And I could glimpse at the woman I was becoming in Act Three. Wise, experienced, and ready to use everything she had learned in service of something larger than herself.

The mirror reflected this truth back at me. Act Three isn't about diminishing. It's about expanding into your fullest glory. Deepening. Using every leaf, every branch, every growth ring you've earned to create something more beautiful than before.

And more than that: it reflected a woman who realized she wasn't alone in this power shift.

The recognition that the framework helping me make sense of my own transition could help millions of women who were standing at the same threshold, wondering if their best days were behind them.

The whisper wasn't just calling me home to myself. It was calling me to help create the community that catches women when they fall through the cracks of cultural expectations about aging, motherhood, and worth.

The woman in the mirror? She wasn't the end of my story.

She was the beginning of our movement.

3

Your Phenomenal Mind

"Finally, brethren, whatsoever things are true, whatsoever things are honest, whatsoever things are just, whatsoever things are pure, whatsoever things are lovely, whatsoever things are of good report; if there be any virtue, and if there be any praise, think on these things."— Philippians 4:8 (KJV)

***

There is a cruel irony of raising children: The day you succeed at teaching them to think for themselves is the day you lose the right to think for them.

I discovered this truth in a crowded coffee shop, sobbing over a letter I never planned to write, mourning the loss of a mind that had never actually belonged to me.

The Assignment That Broke Me Open

What started as a simple school tradition during Charlie's senior year turned into the moment that cracked my heart wide open. The instructions were simple: write a letter to your child, something meaningful to be delivered during their senior retreat. A tradition meant to leave a lasting impression, a milestone wrapped in paper and ink. What I wrote instead was my surrender document.

I remember exactly where I sat, a booth in a crowded coffee shop, with the usual hum of espresso machines and clinking mugs in the background. I opened my notebook and stared at the page, pen in hand, utterly unprepared for what poured out of me.

Nothing was planned. But everything was felt. And what came out wasn't a letter, it was a soul offering.

There are moments in motherhood when wisdom flows through us from somewhere beyond our conscious mind. This letter was one of those moments. My remarkable mind connecting to something greater than myself, channeling truths I didn't even know I carried.

I had written notes to teachers before, including one threatening to remove Charlie from her favorite activity, band, once when the French teacher emailed to complain about her attitude in class. I'd written birthday cards and funny texts to lighten her day. But this? This was different. This wasn't about a grade or a reminder or even a celebration. This was the handing over of everything I had learned through my own wounds and my own healing. Except, I didn't know it at that time. Could not have known.

You don't write something like that casually. Not when you've watched your child grow up through your own tears. Through divorce. Through the shuffling back and forth from mommy's house to daddy's house. Through the shadows of uncertainty and the light of redemption.

And so I wrote.

I remember how my hand trembled slightly. How the coffee grew cold beside me, forgotten. How the world around me, the baristas calling out orders, the customers typing on laptops, the street noise filtering through the windows, all faded into a distant hum. In that moment, there was only the pen, the page, and the fierce, aching love I had for my daughter.

This wasn't the first time I'd tried to capture what I wanted her to know. Over the years, I'd started countless letters, journal entries, unsuccessful attempts to distill decades of living into wisdom she could carry. But something about this moment, the knowledge that she was truly on the cusp of leaving, broke open the dam I'd built around certain truths.

What I gave her was not a perfect set of instructions. It was not a blueprint for success or a roadmap for a flawless life. It was something deeper. From deep within the depths of a mother's heart. An attempt to point her in the direction to accomplish all that I could never accomplish. To soar past any of my accomplishments, past any of my failures. It was a life compass, an echo of all I hoped she would come to believe about herself, God, and the world.

I used to tell her, "If you have a headache, take acetaminophen or ibuprofen, you don't need God for that. But if the dream is HUMONGOUS, if it's so big that you can't possibly achieve it on your own... that's when you know you're dreaming God-sized dreams."

The first battleground and victory ground is the human mind. Win the war there and you are, you will be, victorious. Period. Not because life won't try to knock you off your feet, but because you'll have planted your feet so firmly in truth, to the best of your ability, you'll remember how to stand.

Use your mind to dream big. I mean HUMONGOUS dreams. If your dream doesn't scare you a little or make you doubt whether you're capable, it's too small. Dare to believe the kind of dream that takes God's intervention to bring to life.

Let your imagination soar higher than anyone in your family ever dared to go. Be bold. Be audacious. Be unshakably you.

When you walk into a room, walk like you've already won.

Because victory starts in your mind.

The tears started before I could even finish page one.

Not the gentle, controllable kind that you can dab with a napkin and pretend didn't happen. These were the ugly, soul-deep tears that come from a place so raw you didn't know it existed until someone ripped it open. The kind that make your shoulders shake and your breath come in ragged gasps.

I tried to stop. Tried to pull myself together in this public space where strangers were just trying to enjoy their lattes. But the words kept flowing, and with them, seventeen years of love that had nowhere else to go except onto this paper.

Each sentence was a piece of my heart, torn free and bleeding onto the page. This wasn't just advice from mother to daughter. This was everything I'd learned about how minds grow, how they break free, how they become independent of the very people who shaped them.

This was the conversation I couldn't sit her down to have. The words wouldn't form correctly in person. The message would get lost. I could already picture her asking, "Are you okay, Mom?", if I tried to deliver this face-to-face.

I was so lost in the writing, so completely dissolved into the act of pouring myself out, that I didn't notice the elderly woman approaching my table until she was standing right beside me. "Honey," she said, her voice gentle but firm, "everything's going to be alright." I looked up, tears streaming down my face, probably looking like a woman in the middle of a complete breakdown. Which, I suppose, I was.

She was maybe seventy, with kind eyes and the type of soft, grandmotherly presence that makes you want to confess your deepest fears. Her husband sat watching from their booth, nodding encouragingly, as if they'd agreed between themselves that intervention was necessary.

"I'm sorry," I managed, my voice broken and thick. "I know I'm making a scene. These are... these are happy tears." She tilted her head, studying my face with the wisdom of someone who'd probably comforted crying mothers before. "Are you okay?" she asked, her eyes taking in the notebook, the scattered tissues, the evidence of a heart overflowing.

I nodded, unable to speak for a moment. And when I finally caught my breath, "my daughter," I said incoherently, "writing a letter to my daughter" as if she'd asked for clarification. "I remember," she said simply. "The love gets so big sometimes it has to find a way out."

She squeezed my shoulder once, a gesture so maternal it nearly undid me completely, then returned to her table. But her words stayed with me, echoing in the space between heartbeats: *The love gets so big sometimes it has to find a way out.*

That's exactly what was happening. Seventeen years of loving this child, of watching her grow and change and become someone I helped create but could no longer contain, it was all too much for my body to hold. The letter was the overflow, the spillway for a love too vast for conversation.

What I was really writing about in that space was the emergence of her independent mind. For seventeen years, I had been her primary processor of information. When she was confused, she came to me. When she faced a decision, she sought my counsel, not that we agreed on everything. When the world felt overwhelming, I helped her make sense of it. My mind had been her training wheels, her safety net, her backup hard drive.

But somewhere along the way, particularly during her film classes in high school, she had learned to trust her own analysis over mine. I can pinpoint the exact moment I realized this shift had happened. She'd come home from school, excited about something her film teacher had shared about film and the industry. We got into what I thought was a simple discussion about career prospects, but she quickly turned it into a debate.

I hated that. I hated the talk of film. I disliked the teacher who introduced her to film. Never met the man, just knew I disliked him. Film was not computer science, the college major I had chosen for her long before we started filling college applications. It was one of the first times I can recollect her going against my advice. And I was not an easy mother to go against.

Film is not safe, I argued. Hollywood is not kind to women, much less African-American women. Your success will depend on other people, too many variables, the investors, the industry, and the moviegoers. Even if you manage to pull one off.

Growing up in Nigeria in the 60s and early 80s, there were only three professions worth bragging about: lawyer, doctor, or engineer. Maybe chartered accountant as a distant fourth. These were the careers that made parents beam with pride. Things had changed since the 1980s, of course. I'd been in America for almost thirty years, exposed to countless college degrees and career opportunities. I'd completed both undergraduate and graduate school here. I understood the professional landscape was vast.

Yet when Charlie mentioned film, my Nigerian mindset took over. Jeffrey, my oldest, had even interned in actuarial department at one of my companies. I knew better than to be narrow-minded. But film? To me, that was like saying she wanted to become a gamer. Entertainment, not a real career. Most African parents would have reacted the same way. It sounded like saying you weren't going to school at all. "I've been researching the programs and opportunities. The industry is changing. This isn't a whim, Mom. This is what I want to build my life around."

The way she said it, with such certainty, such conviction, should have been my first warning. This wasn't a child seeking permission. This was a young woman informing me of a decision she'd already made in the privacy of her own mind.

But I was so invested in my vision for her future that I missed the seismic shift happening right in front of me: her mind was learning to operate independently of mine.

She wouldn't, couldn't go against my advice I told myself, I was paying for college so it's going to be computer science unless she managed to secure a full scholarship. I thought the conversation was over. Was I wrong.

Nobody prepares you for this particular parenting paradox: You spend seventeen years teaching them to think critically, then feel betrayed when they think critically about your plans for their lives.

"Use your brain," I must have said to each of my children a thousand times. "There's a reason God gave you a brain. Are you even using it?" I taught them to question. To research. To consider all angles. To make decisions based on facts, not fear. Then my daughter used every single skill I'd given her to dismantle my vision for her future.

We encourage their independence until they become independent of us. We celebrate their decision-making until they make decisions we wouldn't make. We teach them to trust their judgment, then wonder why they've stopped trusting ours above their own.

Her film choice became my education in the betrayal of successful parenting. She was being everything I taught her to be, which sometimes meant becoming someone I didn't expect.

But somewhere in those film class discussions, she had learned to trust her own analysis over mine. She had developed the confidence to disagree with someone she'd spent her entire life looking up to. She had found her voice. The one I encouraged her to find and now was using it to challenge me.

The letter I was writing in that space was my recognition of this shift. I wasn't just encouraging her mind to be remarkable. I was giving myself permission to let it be remarkable without my oversight.

"Your mind is a remarkable tool. Use it" I wrote. Finally acknowledging what she had already been doing for months. The irony wasn't lost on me. I was teaching her to win battles in her mind while fighting my own battle to accept that her mind was now the primary battlefield for her life's decisions.

Growing up with two older brothers had given her advantages I didn't fully appreciate until this moment. Jeffrey, my oldest, was a fierce debater with strong convictions. Bold and confident. He could challenge anyone on any topic without missing a beat. Jason, my middle child, had a gentler approach but was equally convincing in his own way.

Charlie had learned to hold her ground in arguments with both brothers and a mother who made decisions quickly. She'd been trained to present evidence rather than emotions, to stand firm when challenged. Years of family debates had taught her the art of persuasion.

Now all that training was being turned on me.

She researched opportunities with thoroughness that would make any parent proud. She made decisions with careful consideration of all options. She thinks through problems with the same systematic approach she brought to that film class. Ten years later, she still tackles challenges with that same deliberate process.

Charlie went on to Elon University.

We had compromised, her peace offering. A major and a minor. Major in Computer Science, and my world was alright. Minor in Film, my concession. For me, film was still a whim she would outgrow. For her, it must have been a victory. She had gotten me to bend, to see things her way. At least initially.

I thought that was it. Film was a phase, she had outgrown it, seen the errors of her ways and taken my advice.

Wrong!

Well, not directly.

I was in Nigeria. My first trip back in over seventeen years, when the call came. Standing in the humid afternoon heat, attending a friend's mother's funeral, I almost didn't answer the phone. But something about the timing felt urgent.

"Mom, can I schedule time on your calendar for when you return stateside?"

Those words stopped me cold. My daughter and I had developed a code over the years. A way for her to request my full attention instead of my usual rapid-fire responses. She rarely used it. When she did, it meant something big was coming.

I still remember exactly where I stood, rooted in place, afraid. Some memories are etched into your head; this was one of them. Afraid something was wrong, and I was so far from home. Afraid something was wrong, and I was not there to fix it.

"What do you want?" I asked, suddenly afraid. "Ask me now. No need for an appointment."

I couldn't wait to find out what was so important and so urgent that she needed scheduled time to discuss it. My mind immediately went to worst-case scenarios. Something was wrong and I was five thousand miles away, and powerless to fix it.

"Promise me you won't make a decision right away," she pleaded.

"I won't," I lied.

The truth is, I'm incapable of sitting with an issue for any length of time before making a decision. Single parenting conditions you for speed. Quick thinking, faster responses, lightning-fast problem solving. It's survival.

"Well, I've been thinking," she began, and I could hear the careful preparation in her voice. "I've spent almost a year in Computer Science, but film is the direction I would like to go. I would like to transfer."

I was ready with an emphatic NO. But by the time you're raising child number three, exhaustion has a way of tempering your immediate reactions. I bit my tongue long enough to let her continue, even though every word was confirming my worst fears.

Not again. She was bringing up film. Again.

Here I was, five thousand miles away, and she chose this moment to resurrect our old argument about career choices.

"Why?" I managed to ask.

But she wasn't answering my question. She was delivering the presentation she obviously prepared. The one I had forced her to give before she was ready by refusing to wait until I returned home.

"For film. To USC. They have the best film school in the nation, and I think I can get in."

Film? Not again. I must have groaned internally.

"US what?" I interrupted, impatience getting the better of me. My brain was racing, trying to place USC on a map.

"You don't have to do anything," she rushed on, clearly trying to get through her points before I could object with what I'm sure would have been a resounding NO. "I'll complete all the paperwork. Secure the references. All I need is permission to charge the application fee to the emergency credit card you gave me."

And there it was. The ask that had required scheduling time on my calendar.

"Where is USC?" I interjected.

When she spelled it out, my panic intensified. California. The other coast. A mental map of the United States flashed through my mind, showing the vast distance between Maryland and Los Angeles. Five hours by plane instead of the comfortable four-hour drive to Elon I'd grown used to.

My mind raced through the implications. Flight costs. Emergency contacts. Who did I know in Los Angeles. Who could respond if something happened to my daughter? This is how my brain works in crisis mode.

Silence stretched between us while my brain computed all the ways I could say no. Too far. Too expensive. Too unknown. How does USC rank? What are the demographics? Is it even a good school?

But then something unexpected happened. An idea started forming.

She had done what I asked. She went to Elon University. She compromised on the computer science major. She kept her end of our bargain. And now here she was, making her case with the same research skills and logical presentation I spent years teaching her. She must have rehearsed this conversation countless times, refined her arguments, and prepared for my objections.

I forced her hand by demanding an immediate discussion instead of waiting for my return. She wasn't ready, but she was rising to the challenge anyway. The idea crystallized: Good cop, bad cop.

"Okay," I said.

"What? Wait! Did you just say okay?"

The shock in her voice almost made me smile. "Where is my real mom?" she asked.

"I said okay, go ahead."

"Are you serious? You're not going to change your mind, are you?"

"Nope. Won't change my mind."

My brilliant strategy was beautifully simple: good cop, bad cop.

I didn't have enough information to make an informed decision about USC or the transfer process. It was film which still made me uncomfortable. But I could be the good cop. The mother who said yes. The one who didn't stand in the way of her dreams.

After three kids, I had earned the right to forget the college application process. I was done with all that. I would let USC be the bad cop. They would be the ones to reject her. That way, I wouldn't be the mother who crushed her daughter's dreams.

The beauty of the plan? I didn't have to do anything. No applications to review or sign. Just permission to charge a fee to her emergency credit card. We ended that call with her in disbelief and me thinking I dodged the bullet of being the bad mom.

Truth be told, I was convinced USC would turn her down.

I'm sure she was convinced that I would change my mind before she even submitted the application.

I underestimated my daughter.

Months later, we were driving together, her in the passenger seat as always. Her first year at Elon was complete. We were in that in-between space waiting to hear if USC would accept her transfer or if she'd return to Elon in the fall. I'd heard the admission rates for transfers were vanishingly small.

She was scrolling through emails on her phone when she suddenly sat up straight. "That's weird," she said, frowning at her screen. "Why would USC be sending me housing options when they haven't even told me if I'm accepted?" While she puzzled over this apparent administrative error, understanding dawned on me like a lightning strike. I slammed on the brakes so suddenly that the car behind us nearly rear-ended us.

"JoAnna!" I gasped, gripping the steering wheel. "You got in. You did it!"

"But I didn't get an acceptance letter," she protested, still confused.

"What address did you use on your application?" I asked.

"My Elon address..." she replied.

And just like that, our afternoon transformed into a frantic series of calls to what was apparently now her former school, tracking down not just a letter but an entire welcome package.

My brilliant good cop/bad cop strategy had completely backfired. USC wasn't going to be the bad cop after all. They'd said yes to my daughter's dream, which meant I now had to live with mine.

In short, she did exactly what I spent seventeen years teaching her to do. Use your brain. Do your research. Present your best case. No emotions. Present facts.

And that's not a loss. That's transformation.

Her mind didn't need mine to function anymore. But it still wanted mine to witness. The relationship had evolved from dependence to collaboration. From teacher-student to fellow travelers on the journey of life, of growing, of finding our path. From me guiding her thinking to us sharing ideas.

The letter had been my bridge between these two phases, a way to honor the guidance I had given while blessing the independence she claimed.

As you navigate your own transition from primary processor to proud witness, remember what that stranger understood: Sometimes love becomes too big for your body. Sometimes it needs an escape route.

Maybe it's a letter. Maybe it's a journal. Maybe it's a conversation with God in the quiet moments when their independence hits you like a wave. But don't apologize for the tears. Don't contain the overflow. Don't minimize the magnitude of what you're feeling.

You raised a mind capable of thinking beyond yours. You equipped them to question, to research, to trust their own judgment. When they use those skills to chart a course you wouldn't have chosen, that's not rebellion, that's graduation.

The betrayal of successful parenting is this: They become everything you taught them to be, which sometimes means becoming someone you didn't expect.

And your heart, stretched beyond its limits by years of loving them, finally has space to love something else with that same intensity. The woman you're becoming now that your primary job is complete.

The letter was never just about her mind. It was about mine too. About learning to trust it. To use it. To dream with it again.

Because the most beautiful thing about raising a child with an exceptional mind is that they don't just learn to think for themselves. They remind you that it's time to start thinking for yourself again too.

Your Exceptional Mind in the Third Act

Everything we become begins first as a thought, a possibility that we allow ourselves to consider. The Third Act of your life starts the same way, with permission to imagine something new, something that perhaps you've never allowed yourself to consider before.

I think back to when I first dared to dream beyond motherhood again. It wasn't an immediate epiphany after my nest emptied. It was a slow awakening. I'd almost forgotten how to dream for myself, how to envision a future that wasn't centered around my children's needs and schedules.

For months, I carried around a journal, mostly empty except for practical lists and occasional reflections on my children's new adult lives. But slowly, other words began to appear on those pages.

Dreams. Ideas. Possibilities. The faintest outlines of ambitions I'd packed away decades ago.

"What if I finally wrote that book?"

"What if I started a small business?"

"What if I went back to school?"

Questions about what I wanted to do with the rest of my life that had nothing to do with managing anyone else's. Thoughts about interests I had abandoned. Skills I had never developed. Experiences I had postponed until "someday when I have time."

At first, these thoughts felt almost illicit, selfish even. Who was I to want more at this stage? Hadn't I already lived a full life? Wasn't it enough to have raised children, to have supported a family, to have weathered storms and celebrated joys?

But the thoughts persisted, gentle but insistent. And I began to recognize them not as selfish indulgences but as sacred invitations. Divine nudges asking me to remember who I was, not just as a mother, but as a woman with gifts, passions, and purpose that extended beyond the roles I had played.

Recognition is where transformation begins. Recognizing the power of your own mind to shape your experience. To recognize that the voice in your head. The one that speaks limitations and fears is not the only voice you can listen to. There is another voice, deeper and truer, that reminds you of who you really are and what you're capable of becoming.

This recognition doesn't happen all at once. It comes in glimpses. In moments when you catch yourself thinking differently, seeing possibilities where once you saw only obligations.

Transformation isn't linear or crystal clear. It doesn't shout. It whispers, it nudges, and if you allow it, it carries you to a place you may never have imagined, but always longed for.

You'll move between dreams and doubts. One day feeling certain about your new direction, the next questioning everything. There's a messy middle where grief reappears just when you think you've made peace with your children's independence. They visit for a holiday, and when they start packing to leave, that familiar ache returns. There will be moments when you doubt your discoveries about yourself.

But then, bit by bit, the hesitancy lifts. You notice that the doubts you once clung to don't hold the same weight. The expectations that shaped your life feel a little less binding. It's not always pretty, and sometimes it's messy, but it's deeply human.

Each woman's transformation is personal, shaped by her unique circumstances. Work, health, relationships, financial realities, her interests. It's not a destination but an evolving journey.

Transformation, in truth, feels less like becoming someone new and more like returning to yourself. Not erased by years of responsibility, but revealed through them. It doesn't roar; it hums. It reminds you that this stage of life is not about winding down, but about finally opening up - to possibility, to joy, to the life you can still choose.

So begin here. With your thoughts. With your beliefs. With the dreams that still call when you're brave enough to listen. At first, you test it. You say no and the world doesn't fall apart. You say yes and feel something wake inside you. Over time, the hesitancy eases. The dutiful voice that once dictated your choices grows quieter, and the softer voice - the one that asks, What do you want? - grows stronger.

Your remarkable mind doesn't retire when your children leave home. It just gets a terrifying new assignment: figuring out who you're supposed to become next. It isn't limited by age or circumstance or even by past disappointments. It remains, at this very moment, your most powerful ally in becoming the woman you were always meant to be.

Welcome to your exceptional mind.

4

Slipping Through My Fingers

"If I take the wings of the morning, and dwell in the uttermost parts of the sea; Even there shall thy hand lead me, and thy right hand shall hold me." — *Psalm 139:9-10 (KJV)*

***

The reality of letting go is that it doesn't happen once. It happens in three devastating stages, each one designed to destroy you in a completely different way. Each death arrives disguised as something else, celebration, routine, success, so you never see the blade coming until it has already pierced your heart.

But here's what they don't tell you about those three deaths. They're not the end of your story. They're the beginning of something you never saw coming. A transformation so profound it will make you question everything you thought you knew about power, purpose, and what it means to be a woman in this world.

Death #1: The Euphoria

First comes the high that feels like victory. High school graduation arrives like a ticker-tape parade when they're eighteen (or in our case, seventeen), and you're both the grand marshal and the cheering crowd. Look what you've accomplished! Look what you've raised!

You plan graduation parties with the manic energy of someone trying to hold onto time. You order announcements like they're legal documents proving your success. You pose for pictures with a smile so wide it makes your cheekbones ache. Desperate to capture proof that this moment, this pinnacle, actually happened.

You're riding the high of their achievement as if it's your own, because for all those years, it has been your own.

Every A+ paper has your fingerprints on it. The late nights you spent hunched over the kitchen table explaining fractions until they clicked. Drying tears over difficult concepts that made your child feel stupid until you convinced them they were brilliant. Every college acceptance letter validates not just their potential but your parenting, as if the admissions committee was also grading your motherhood. Every milestone they've reached was constructed on a foundation you poured with your own hands, mixed with your own tears, reinforced with your own prayers.

This is the stage where you still get to claim partial credit. Where "we got into college" still feels natural rolling off your tongue. Where your neighbors congratulate you as much as they congratulate your child. Where their success story and your mothering story are so intertwined you can't tell where one ends and the other begins.

The euphoria is intoxicating because you're still essential to every decision. Which dorm bedding will make them feel at home in a place that isn't home? What laptop specs will carry them through four years of learning you can't guide? How many towels does independence require? You're the project manager of their independence. The logistics coordinator of their future. You're busy. Needed. Important.

Your phone buzzes constantly with questions that make your heart sing because they still need your input. You research and compare and analyze like their future depends on your thoroughness, which, in your mind, it does.

Back in the space, writing through tears that wouldn't stop, I felt all of this crashing over me again. The pen moved across the page as if it had a mind of its own, documenting not just my love for her but my terror at her independence. The tears started somewhere around the second page. Not the gentle, controllable kind that you can dab with a napkin and pretend didn't happen.

These were the ugly, soul-deep tears that come from a place so raw you didn't know it existed until someone ripped it open. The kind that make your shoulders shake and your breath come in ragged gasps.

Nobody mentions how loving someone with your whole heart is that sometimes your heart becomes too full for your body to contain. I tried to stop. Tried to pull myself together in this public space where strangers were just trying to enjoy their lattes. But the words kept flowing, and with them, seventeen years of love that had nowhere else to go except onto this paper.

Each sentence was a piece of my heart, torn free and bleeding onto the page. This wasn't just advice from mother to daughter. This was the distilled essence of everything I'd learned about minds. How they grow, how they break free, how they become independent of the very people who shaped them.

The stranger's kindness in that space reminded me of something essential: This overwhelming love wasn't meant to be contained. It was meant to be shared, expressed, poured out without apology. Some truths are too big for conversation but perfect for paper. Some love is too deep for daily interaction but essential for lasting connection. Some wisdom can only be transmitted when the receiver can't interrupt, can't deflect, can't escape the full weight of what's being offered.

The letter became my gift to her developing mind, not instructions on how to think, but encouragement to think boldly. Not a map for her future, but confidence in her ability to chart her own course.

But writing it was also a gift to myself. It was my way of honoring both the mother I had been and the woman I was evolving into. The woman who could celebrate her daughter's independence instead of mourning her own obsolescence.

As I wrote about her remarkable mind, I was also rediscovering mine. For too long, I had defined my intelligence by how well I could anticipate and meet others' needs. I measured my mental capacity by how efficiently I could solve their problems, manage their schedules, and facilitate their dreams.

Twenty-plus years of believing that my intellectual value was measured only by how well I served others' minds, never my own. As if a woman's intelligence was only legitimate when it was in service to someone else's dreams. But the mind that had guided three children through their formative years was finally free to begin guiding its owner toward her own transformation.

I wondered how many other women were sitting in such spaces, realizing that the minds they'd used to raise brilliant children had been temporarily redirected, not permanently diminished. How many of us had forgotten that our exceptional minds were still exceptional, even when they weren't actively mothering? I began to understand that the remarkable mind I had celebrated in my daughter was the same exceptional mind that lived within me. It had simply been redirected for so long toward other people's development that I'd forgotten it could serve my own.

This transition steals more than children from your house, it leaves you with acres of mental space you don't know how to fill. Suddenly, all that processing power you've been using to manage their lives is available for your own dreams again.

You're also completely unprepared for the crash coming next.

Death #2: The Awakening

Then comes the crash that masquerades as normalcy.

The reality is that college drop-off day isn't the hard part. The hard part is the Tuesday morning a week later, when you forget and call upstairs for someone who isn't there. The hard part is standing in the grocery store aisle, your hand hovering over their favorite cereal, before remembering with a physical jolt that you don't need to buy it anymore.

I discovered this truth standing barefoot on cold asphalt at 6:30 AM, chasing a garbage truck in my pajamas while calling "Charlie!", my daughter's nickname, into the dawn air that swallowed my voice like it had never existed.

The first time the trash truck came after she left for college, I heard it from blocks away. Every parent knows that sound, the hydraulic wheezing, the mechanical grinding that breaks the morning quiet like a timekeeper announcing another day of routines that no longer make sense.

For years, that trash truck had been OUR responsibility. Part of the invisible architecture of our shared life. She'd complained about it every single Tuesday, dragged her feet down the driveway, groaned when I called her name from the kitchen window. But it was ours. We were a team. A system. A family that functioned together, our lives interlocked like puzzle pieces that created something beautiful and whole.

And now there was just me. Standing barefoot on cold asphalt that bit through my thin pajama soles, clutching a plastic bin like it was a lifeline to a life that had already sailed away without me.

The sanitation worker paused in his mechanical routine, clearly uncomfortable with my display of raw emotion spilling across the suburban morning. "You okay, ma'am?" His voice carried the gentle concern of someone who had witnessed breakdown before.

I tried to nod, tried to wave him off with the casual dismissal of someone who had their life together, but my throat had closed around words I couldn't form. The tears were coming whether I authorized them or not, hot and relentless and completely beyond my control. "My daughter," I managed, my voice cracking on the words like ice under pressure. "She's at college now. This was... I forgot... I haven't had to remember the trash myself in a long time.."

The words hung in the morning air, ridiculous and profound simultaneously. Who breaks down over garbage pickup? Who sobs in their pajamas over household chores? But his expression softened with recognition that nearly undid me completely. Maybe he was a father. Maybe he had stood in driveways watching his own children disappear into futures he helped create but couldn't control. Maybe he had seen enough suburban mothers having their private moments of reckoning to understand that grief wears many disguises.

"Gets easier," he said gently, and there was such kindness in those two words that I wanted to hug this stranger who'd accidentally witnessed my heart breaking over municipal waste management.

He continued down the street with the mechanical efficiency of someone who'd witnessed a thousand small heartbreaks disguised as ordinary Tuesday mornings, leaving me standing there in my pajamas. Finally understanding something my friends had been trying to tell me with their knowing looks and gentle warnings.

They don't make a switch for a mother's heart, no dimmer to gradually reduce the love, no timer to ease the transition from essential to optional. A mother's heart doesn't understand phases and timetables the way the world insists it should. It keeps showing up at full wattage, even when the room has already emptied, even when the need for that light has quietly shifted somewhere else.

Letting go wasn't going to be a single moment of brave release. The kind you see in movies where mothers wave handkerchiefs and smile through tears as their children board trains to better lives. It was going to be a thousand small deaths like this one, routine moments that suddenly became monuments to everything that had changed while I wasn't paying attention.

But in that stranger's simple words - "gets easier" - something else was being born. I couldn't name it then, standing there in my pajamas with yesterday's mascara streaking down my cheeks. It was hope. Not the bright, shiny kind that promises everything will go back to the way it was, but the quiet, steady kind that suggests you might survive this. That there might be something on the other side of this grief that doesn't require you to stay broken forever.

Death #3: The Reckoning

The third death cuts deepest: The day you realize they're not just gone, they're thriving without you.

Your child's success without your daily intervention feels simultaneously like your greatest achievement and your most devastating loss. It's the cruelest victory imaginable, proof that you succeeded so completely at your job that you've worked yourself out of it.

This death arrived through a phone call on a Wednesday evening when I was standing at my kitchen sink, washing dishes for one. Charlie's voice came through the speaker bright with excitement about a class project, animated in ways I hadn't heard since she was small and breathless with stories about playground adventures.

She was telling me about projects I didn't understand, using terms I'd never heard. Describing mentors I had never met who were guiding her through opportunities I couldn't facilitate. Her voice carried the particular energy of someone building something meaningful. Someone evolving into someone she was proud to be.

She was growing into everything I'd raised her to be, which turned out to be someone who didn't need me anymore.

The conversation lasted around twenty minutes, but I heard every word through the filter of my own irrelevance. She talked about late nights studies that I couldn't ease with hot chocolate and shoulder rubs or hugs. She mentioned weekend volunteer work where she was networking with people whose names I'd never know. She described being part of a school sponsored safe free ride program on weekends with friends who would become her chosen family while I remained her inherited past. And then I understood the cruel mathematics of successful motherhood. The better you are at your job, the more completely you eliminate your position.

I hung up the phone feeling proud and hollowed out in equal measure. She was using skills I helped develop but couldn't direct anymore. She was living my values but not my involvement. She was everything I'd dreamed she could be, which was someone who could dream without me. This was the beautiful betrayal of successful parenting, raising someone so capable, so independent, so self-sufficient that they prove your love by no longer needing it.

Back inside after my trash truck breakdown, I made coffee with hands that still trembled slightly from crying on the curb like a woman who'd lost her mind along with her purpose. The morning coffee ritual became its own grief.

For years, she made my coffee exactly how I liked it, she was only fifteen or so when she started. Too young to drink it herself, but she knew my preferences better than I did. Cream, no sugar, stirred (her quirky addition that somehow made it taste better). She would bring it to me in my favorite mug, whichever one that happened to be that week, but somehow it always tasted better when she made it.

Now I stood in my kitchen, fumbling with measurements like a guest in my own home, adding too much cream, then too little, trying to recreate the alchemy she had performed without thinking. The coffee tasted wrong no matter what I did. Not because of the ratios, but because it was missing the ingredient of care from hands that knew me that well.

The thing about the empty nest is that you don't just miss your child. You miss the version of yourself that existed when they needed you. You miss being the person who mattered that much to someone that important.

The first week she was gone, I forgot to do laundry entirely. It had been her chore for years. Part of the life skills I was supposedly teaching her for independence. I didn't realize my oversight until I was down to my last clean clothes, standing in my closet like a woman who had forgotten how to be an adult.

When I called to tell her, she laughed, not unkindly, but with the easy dismissal of someone who had already moved on to new responsibilities while I was still learning to navigate the basics of my reorganized existence. "Well, Mom, looks like you'll have to figure that out now." Her laughter was loving but matter-of-fact, the sound of someone who had already integrated this lesson while I was still taking the test.

This is something few people understand about intensive motherhood: we don't just raise children; we absorb them into our daily existence until we can't tell where we end and they begin. Our identities become so enmeshed with theirs that separation feels like amputation.

Heritage Collision

But it wasn't just the physical absence I was mourning. The deeper grief was existential - the collision between the woman I was raised to be and the woman American parenting had required me to become. My Nigerian heritage whispered that mothers become more essential with age, while my American reality celebrated making myself obsolete.

Being an African mother raising American children means you spend years preparing them for a kind of independence that your soul was never designed to understand.

I should have been proud. I was proud. But I was also grieving something that my heritage had never prepared me to lose: the certainty that family stays family, that children remain children, that mothers remain essential until their dying day.

My daughter was living the American dream, complete independence, self-sufficiency, building a life that belonged entirely to her. But my African heart was mourning the loss of community-centered living, the death of the extended family model where wisdom and proximity go hand in hand.

Here I was, being congratulated for successfully making myself unnecessary, while every cell in my body screamed that something fundamental was wrong with this picture. The congratulations felt hollow, like praise for a job I never wanted to complete.

I began to recognize this feeling as something deeper than personal grief. This was systematic displacement, being praised for succeeding at something that violated every instinct I'd inherited about what motherhood should look like. This was living in cultural exile, applauded for outcomes that left me feeling emptied rather than accomplished.

But then something started shifting in ways I couldn't have predicted.

It was subtle at first, like dawn breaking so gradually you don't notice until suddenly there's light where darkness used to live. The world was moving along in spite of my grief, and that felt both insulting and oddly liberating. I was still going to work every day, fielding the well-meaning questions about how she was adjusting, how I was coping. Initially, I delivered the standard responses with the automatic efficiency of someone who'd mastered the art of public composure.

But then came the revolutionary realization: I no longer had to fly down I-95 for school pickups. No more calculating drive times against meeting schedules. No more mental gymnastics around who needed to be where when.

For the first time in over twenty years, my time belonged to me.

I started with baby steps, like someone learning to walk again after a long illness. A movie on a Tuesday night without checking anyone's schedule. Grocery shopping that meandered instead of marched. Books read without interruption. These small freedoms felt both thrilling and terrifying, like stepping into a room I'd forgotten existed in my own house.

But it was Houston that became the real awakening.

Houston: The City That Taught Me I Still Had a Runway

When I moved to Houston, I arrived as anonymous as a woman could be. No history. No predetermined roles. No one who knew me as anyone's mother. In Maryland, I'd been tethered to suburban rhythms and the accumulated weight of over twenty years of being someone specific to specific people. But Houston was different. Houston was a transplant city, where most everyone you meet carries the particular energy of starting over somewhere new.

It was perfect for someone like me. Someone discovering who she was when she wasn't responsible for orchestrating anyone else's existence.

I've always been drawn to strangers, comfortable with the small conversations that bloom in grocery store lines and coffee shop queues. In Houston, these casual encounters became something more deliberate. I started meeting other women in various states of transition, divorce, empty nest, career change, reinvention. People will share their stories if you offer them the gift of genuine attention, and I discovered I was particularly skilled at creating space for women to voice things they'd never said out loud.

Slowly, the revelation dawned: I was not alone in this particular wilderness.

Houston offered itself generously to anyone willing to engage. Meetup groups, Eventbrite announcements, community calendars thick with possibility. There was always something happening, and the more I showed up, the more women I encountered wrestling with that universal question: What Now? What comes next?

But showing up wasn't always smooth. I had to learn the difference between genuine community and networking opportunities disguised as friendship.

Rising Tide Reality Check

The Rising Tide Society meeting was my first real networking event in Houston. I found the Houston chapter through their Facebook group, introduced myself as a relocating photographer, and received warm responses that felt like exactly what I needed.

The monthly meetup was at a popular spot in the Heights, and I arrived early, camera bag in hand, ready to document the evening and hopefully make real connections. The energy was exactly what I'd hoped for - creative women supporting each other, sharing resources, celebrating wins.

That's when I met her, the "influencer" whose name I've gratefully forgotten. She was magnetic in the way people are when they know how to work a room, moving from conversation to conversation with practiced ease.

"You're the photographer who just moved from Maryland!" she said, lighting up when someone introduced us. "I've been looking at your work online. It's beautiful."

We talked about my transition to Houston, the challenges of building a client base in a new city. She was warm, asking thoughtful questions about my background, my style, my hopes for building community here.

"I have this amazing project coming up," she said toward the end of the evening. "A brand collaboration event. I'd love to have you photograph it. It would be such great exposure - I have thousands of followers who are always looking for photographers."

I should have asked more questions right then. Should have discussed rates, expectations, deliverables. But I was new, eager to connect, and still operating under that Maryland mindset where community meant mutual support. When someone in your network needed something, you helped if you could.

"I'd love to," I said, and we exchanged contact information.

Three weeks later, I found myself at her actual event, an elaborate brand collaboration she'd staged at an upscale venue. The setup was impressive - perfectly curated displays, branded everything, every detail designed for social media perfection.

For three hours, I shot every angle she requested. The products, the interactions, the carefully posed moments with other influencers and brand representatives. I worked the room professionally, capturing the energy and atmosphere she'd envisioned.

When dinner was served, I realized with crushing clarity that there was no plate for me. No seat reserved. No place at the table I'd spent the evening documenting. I was the help, not the guest. The photographer, not the participant.

Standing in that beautifully lit room, watching people I'd just photographed enjoy conversation and community I wasn't invited to join, I felt the particular humiliation of someone who'd confused kindness with friendship, work with welcome.

But here's what Rising Tide Society actually gets right: community over competition. When I shared this experience (carefully, without naming names) at the next monthly meeting, the response was immediate and supportive. Other photographers shared similar stories. Veterans offered guidance about contracts and boundaries. The real community rallied around the lesson.

I made two decisions driving home from that brand event. First, I'd strategically watermark every image where it couldn't be cropped out. Second, I'd ask probing questions before saying yes. Win-win or no deal.

That woman did me a favor, though she'll never know it. She taught me the difference between being used and being useful. More importantly, she helped me recognize the difference between networking opportunists and genuine community builders.

Some of the photographers I met through Rising Tide became lasting friends who've supported my work for years. The real community welcomed me with open arms and taught me that true collaboration looks nothing like exploitation disguised as opportunity.

Sometimes the most valuable lessons come wrapped in the worst experiences.

The Miller Outdoor Theater in Hermann park became my accidental classroom. I'd arrive with packed picnic, folding chair and a blanket, expecting nothing more than evening entertainment, but consistently found myself in conversations that lasted long after the music ended. These weren't casual acquaintanceships, they were connections forged by shared understanding, women recognizing themselves in each other's stories.

The more I engaged, the more my voice returned to me. Not the voice that managed family logistics or mediated teenage drama, but the voice that had always existed underneath all those necessary roles.

I was making friends, but more than that, I was making a difference. Casual conversations evolved into coffee dates, which deepened into informal mentoring sessions where I found myself offering perspective earned through years of navigating challenges these women were just beginning to face.

The realization hit me like a revelation: I was not as powerless as I thought.

I missed Charlie, desperately, daily, in ways that still caught me off guard, but I was also discovering something profound. The runway of my life was still long, stretching far beyond the mothering years I'd assumed would define me completely. I could see pieces of myself reflected in these women, decades of accumulated wisdom, hard-won experience, practical knowledge about surviving and thriving through life's inevitable transitions.

The Economic Awakening

And then came the revelation that reframed everything: the economic awakening that arrived not as theory but as lived reality.

For the first time in decades, the money in my account was entirely mine to direct. No more splitting resources across multiple needs, no more calculating whether this expense meant sacrificing that opportunity for someone else. The endless stream of tuition payments, school fees, extracurricular costs, and general child-rearing expenses that had channeled my income in predetermined directions for over twenty years, suddenly, those channels were mine to redirect.

Travel, which had been relegated to the realm of "someday" dreams, became immediate possibility. Not family vacations requiring coordination of multiple schedules and preferences, but travel chosen purely for my own curiosity and pleasure. The liberation was intoxicating, to book a flight based solely on where I wanted to go, when I wanted to go, without consulting anyone else's calendar or budget.

But it was more than financial freedom. It was temporal freedom, the luxury of making decisions without factoring in family logistics. I could attend evening events without arranging childcare or worry about coming home late. I could travel spontaneously without ensuring someone else's needs were covered in my absence. My schedule belonged to me in ways I'd forgotten were possible.

Houston amplified this awakening. In Maryland, I'd been embedded in a web of roles and responsibilities, community obligations, church commitments, school involvement, the accumulated identity of twenty plus years of being someone's mother in a place where everyone knew exactly who that made me.

But Houston offered me the gift of anonymity. I was just Ronnie. Period. No modifying titles, no inherited expectations, no predetermined place in anyone else's story.

The exhale was profound, like finally releasing a breath I'd been holding for over two decades.

As I moved through Houston's social and small business landscape, I began recognizing this same transformation in other women. They weren't just attending events; they were investing in themselves with the particular enthusiasm of people who'd rediscovered they had selves worth investing in. Workshops and classes chosen for pure interest rather than practical necessity. Travel planned around personal dreams rather than family obligations. Real estate investments made with the confidence of women who'd learned to trust their own judgment.

I found myself in conversations with women who were making inroads into traditionally male-dominated spaces, not because they'd suddenly gained expertise, but because they'd finally gained the time and financial autonomy to pursue interests that had been deferred for decades.

The realization dawned slowly, then all at once: We weren't just individual women figuring out our next chapters. We represented massive collective economic power that had been largely invisible because it had been channeled through family obligations for so long.

The Universal Truth About Transitions

What I discovered in Houston transcended empty nest syndrome. I'd stumbled upon a universal principle that governs any major life transition, divorce, career change, loss, any seismic shift that leaves you wondering who you are when you're not who you used to be.

I'd learned this truth first during my divorce, though I hadn't recognized it as transferable wisdom at the time. My parents had divorced, and I'd carried the naive certainty that it couldn't happen to me. When it did, I felt like I was drowning in waters I'd never imagined navigating.

The world kept spinning while mine had shattered, and that felt like a personal insult. Why was everyone else moving forward with their lives while I was barely treading water? Grief operates with this particular cruelty, it makes you feel simultaneously invisible and utterly exposed, convinced that your pain should pause the universe while simultaneously angry that it doesn't.

I had a work friend, Jeff, who recognized something in my careful composure and invited me on daily walks through downtown DC. Some days we talked; others we simply moved through the city together, my anguish given space to exist without requiring management or resolution.

He was the only person I couldn't lie to with my automatic "I'm fine" response.

Through those walks, I learned that major life transitions have their own physics. You can fight against the disorientation, expending enormous energy trying to control the spinning, or you can learn to move with it until the motion slows naturally. Like seeds that must winter underground before they can grow, some experiences simply must run their course.

The key insight came later, through a divorce support group where I met women in various stages of rebuilding. One woman, heavily medicated and barely present due to the trauma of losing her family and marriage simultaneously, still possessed enough presence of mind to offer advice to those of us earlier in the process.

"Buy plants," she told me. "All that energy you've been pouring into taking care of everyone else, channel it into something green and growing."

I'd always killed plants, but suddenly my brown thumb transformed. Every ounce of nurturing energy that had nowhere to land found purpose in coaxing life from soil and seeds.

The universal principle became clear: No matter what transition you're navigating, the world continues its rotation. People move forward with their lives. Time passes whether you participate or resist. But within that apparent indifference lies opportunity, the chance to redirect energy that's been channeled in one direction toward purposes you've never had space to explore.

Every woman in that support group arrived carrying a specific grief, but our collective revelation was identical: We were more than the roles we'd lost. The titles might change, but the person underneath remained, often more clearly visible once the demands of those roles no longer obscured her.

The Movement Moment: When Individual Healing Became Collective Power

Photography had always been more than hobby for me, it was a way of seeing, of capturing truth that existed beneath surface presentation. But in Houston, it became something unexpected: a lens through which I could witness and document a quiet revolution happening among women my age.

I'd joined an online photography group that issued monthly challenges and chose the theme "Cover Girl" during one of those challenges. I knew almost immediately what I wanted to explore.

My demographic would be women over fifty, because no matter your age, you deserve to see yourself as cover-worthy.

What started as an artistic project became an accidental anthropological study. To photograph someone authentically, you have to know them, and to know them, you have to listen. Really listen. As I conducted pre-shoot interviews with these women, I began hearing the same themes echoing across different stories: the need to belong, the search for identity beyond traditional roles, the hunger to be seen for who they were becoming rather than who they'd always been.

These weren't just individual conversations; they were variations on a universal theme. I was witnessing the collective thread of pain that connected us, but also the shared yearning for something beyond healing, for recognition, for purpose, for the right to remain vital and relevant in a culture that often treats women over fifty as invisible.

The photo reveal night was transformative, for them and for me. I watched women see themselves through my lens, capturing not just their appearance but the essence of how they'd described themselves during our conversations. The joy was profound, almost spiritual. One woman told me she hadn't been professionally photographed since childhood because she'd been too busy photographing everyone else, her children, their milestones, their achievements, leaving no visual record of her own evolution.

"I didn't want the night to end," she told me afterward. "I felt so beautiful, so seen. I couldn't just go home, I had to go somewhere and be this person you showed me I was."

My friend Raquel organized a gallery night, transforming the reveal into a celebration with black and gold elegance that honored these women as the works of art they were. Watching their families and friends marvel at these portraits, I realized something profound was happening. This wasn't just about individual confidence, it was about shifting narratives, challenging assumptions, creating new visual language for what power and beauty looked like in the Third Act.

Each conversation had revealed the same pattern: women with decades of accumulated wisdom, financial resources, and hard-won perspective, sitting in a cultural blind spot that pretended they didn't exist until they needed assisted living.

This wasn't personal healing anymore. This was a movement waiting to happen.

The Business Case for Forgotten Women

The economic reality became impossible to ignore once I learned to see it clearly. Our society has created comprehensive support systems for every life stage except one: There are programs for babies, initiatives for children, resources for teens, guidance for young adults, career development for professionals in their prime, and then there's a vast, inexplicable gap that leaps directly to retirement planning and senior living, as if women between fifty and seventy simply don't exist.

Yet this supposedly invisible demographic controls enormous economic power - 73 million women worldwide standing at the threshold of their highest earning potential, their peak investment years, their maximum wealth-building decades. Women who control $15 trillion in global wealth, with disposable income, accumulated wealth, and decades of decision-making experience, sitting in a market vacuum that pretends we've vanished until we're old enough to need medical alert systems. Women entering their third act where they finally get to spend their money on their own dreams instead of everyone else's needs.

The irony is staggering. Men have built-in social infrastructure, golf courses, sports bars, professional networks that seamlessly transition from business networking to retirement fellowship. But women? We're expected to navigate this life stage without roadmaps, support systems, or even acknowledgment that we exist as a distinct market with specific needs and considerable purchasing power.

In Houston, I was witnessing the early stirrings of women creating their own solutions, informal networks, self-organized groups, word-of-mouth recommendations for everything from financial advisors who understood their specific circumstances to travel companies that catered to their newly liberated schedules.

We weren't just individual women making personal adjustments. We were a massive, underserved demographic beginning to recognize our collective influence.

The Sacred Exchange

I feel, with my whole being, that nobody prepares you for the series of changes you'll experience, sometimes simultaneously: You lose your daily purpose, but you gain your life back. You lose being needed, but you discover being wanted. You lose control over their choices, but you gain freedom over your own.

The love doesn't become smaller when they leave, it becomes too big for your body, expanding beyond the boundaries of daily care and transforming into something that can travel across states, across time zones, across the growing distance between who they were and who they're becoming.

Standing in that amphitheater in Houston, surrounded by women discovering themselves in their second and third acts, I finally understood that this isn't about replacement, it's about integration. The Third Act isn't about starting over; it's about finally having the space to become who you always were underneath all the roles and responsibilities.

Discovering that the love that feels too vast for one heart creates space for new dreams, new communities, new expressions of purpose.

But what I learned in Houston is that millions of women are discovering what I discovered, that when your children no longer need your daily attention, you don't become irrelevant. You become available. Available for purposes you never had time to pursue. Available for relationships you never had space to nurture. Available for dreams you never had permission to chase.

The Hope Hidden in the Breakdown

Looking back at that garbage truck moment, I can see now what was being born in that breakdown that I couldn't recognize then. In that stranger's simple words, it gets easier", something profound was planted. Not confidence, exactly, but peace. The deep peace that comes from realizing you're going to survive this, that there's something on the other side of the grief that doesn't require you to stay broken forever.

I'm sure that the sanitation worker was just being kind to a disheveled woman who'd rolled out like an unmade bed, disrupting his clockwork route with suburban drama. His job was time-sensitive, so many houses to reach, so many bins to empty within a finite schedule. Other than giving him a frightening sight, I'm sure he wasn't thinking seriously about my existential crisis.

But I felt power and hope in his words. While it didn't plug the hole in my heart, it stopped the gushing. It gave me something to hold onto during one the darkest moments of that transition, the simple faith that time would teach me to carry this differently.

What was being born in that moment was the recognition that love doesn't end when it's no longer needed in familiar ways. It evolves. It finds new expressions. It discovers new purposes.

The Slipping Into Soaring

Here's the truth about things slipping through your fingers: Sometimes what feels like losing your grip is actually learning to let go.

For seventeen years, I had held on so tightly, to schedules and routines, to roles and responsibilities, to the beautiful weight of being needed every single day. My fingers were cramped from gripping, my heart exhausted from holding.

The slipping wasn't my failure. It was physics. It was design. It was the natural result of love that knows how to release what it has nurtured.

Standing at my kitchen window, watching my car keys in the same spot I drop it everyday, no borrowing my car for a quick errand or outing, I finally understood what that sanitation worker meant when he said "it gets easier."

He didn't mean the missing would stop. He meant I would learn to carry it differently. That the love wouldn't diminish, but it would transform. That the connection wouldn't break, but it would evolve. That someday I would understand the difference between loving someone close and loving someone free.

But here's what slipped through my fingers in the most beautiful way possible: The illusion that successful motherhood meant being needed forever.

What I caught in return was something I never expected: Permission to need myself again. Permission to want things for myself again. Permission to build something meaningful from everything I'd learned along the way.

And the revelation that millions of women just like me were catching the same thing, discovering that this overwhelming love doesn't disappear when they leave. It transforms. It finds new purposes to serve. New communities to nurture.

We weren't slipping into irrelevance. We were slipping into our power.

We weren't disappearing into empty nests. We were emerging into economic force, collective wisdom, and untapped potential that the world hadn't learned to see yet.

And there's a particular kind of beauty in love that's brave enough to applaud the very independence it taught but never wanted to need, and wise enough to build something meaningful from everything it learned along the way.

5

What They Don't Tell You At Drop-off

"Be strong and of a good courage, fear not, nor be afraid of them: for the Lord thy God, he it is that doth go with thee; he will not fail thee, nor forsake thee." — *Deuteronomy 31:6 (KJV)*

***

This ancient wisdom that anchored me through my daughter's departure speaks to something every parent feels in their bones, the sacred rhythm of holding on and letting go. Whether you find this truth in scripture, in nature's seasons, or in your own understanding of life's patterns, the principle remains: everything has its time, including the time to release what we love most.

Drop-off day carries a secret. You're not just saying goodbye to your child. You're saying goodbye to the woman you've been for the past seventeen years.

You spend seventeen years teaching them to need us less, then act shocked when they don't need us anymore. The real tragedy of drop-off day isn't that our children are leaving, it's that we never prepared ourselves to stay.

The Illusion of Readiness

The drive to Elon felt familiar, almost routine. This was my third college drop-off. I'd done this with her brothers before, just at different schools - and Charlie and I had already visited Elon for orientation, so this felt like well-worn territory. We were both animated, excited even, she'd already connected with her roommate and bandmates online, so it felt less like she was leaving for the unknown and more like she was heading to meet friends.

If she was anxious, she didn't let it show. And I was somewhat giddy at becoming an empty nester, little did I know it was only in theory. We were both oblivious to the fact that this drive was different. This time, when we reached our destination, I'd be driving home alone. All that preparation, all that confident energy? It was just elaborate emotional procrastination.

We focused on the logistics because the emotional reality is too big to face: We've been unconsciously training ourselves out of a job for two decades, then wonder why unemployment feels like death.

Think about it. Every milestone we celebrate, first steps, first day of school, first time driving alone, is actually them needing us a little bit less. We cheer their independence while secretly mourning our own obsolescence. We raise them to fly away, then stand in empty driveways wondering why we feel so grounded.

The cruelest irony? The better we parent, the less they need us. Success in motherhood is measured by how well we eliminate our own necessity. Think about that for a moment. What other job measures success by how quickly you can make yourself irrelevant? What other role celebrates the complete elimination of your own importance? We've been conditioned to see this as noble sacrifice when it's actually systematic erasure masquerading as good parenting.

When You Birthed Them, You Didn't Know You Were Also Birthing Your Surrender

The first night after we dropped her off, I woke at 2 a.m. to check my phone. No texts. No calls. No emergencies. Just the soft glow of the screen telling me she was fine without me.

I stared at her contact photo, her smiling face, caught mid-laugh on a beach trip the summer before, and wondered if she was sleeping. If her roommate snored. If she remembered to plug in her phone. If she was lonely.

That first night reveals something unexpected, it's not about missing them. It's about the devastating realization that they're not missing you, or you have no way of knowing if they are missing you just as much as you're missing them, hoping, wishing you could hold them, hug them, just one more time.

I typed out three different messages, deleted them all, and finally settled on a simple heart emoji. Sent it. Watched as "Delivered" appeared beneath it. No immediate response. No blue bubbles typing back. Just silence. I put the phone down and stared at the ceiling, counting the hours until morning when I could reasonably text again without seeming desperate.

This, I realized, was what letting go felt like, not a single moment, but a thousand small surrenders, one text at a time.

The Cultural Collision at the Core

American parenting culture hides this truth. We are the only culture in the world that celebrates making ourselves obsolete. My Nigerian heritage created an entirely different lens on Charlie's departure. In most African homes, especially Nigeria, college is as non-negotiable as elementary school. It's not a question of if, but when and where. Most African children start school earlier, as I did, so Charlie leaving at barely seventeen felt perfectly normal to us, even though it shocked her American friends' parents.

When I shared the news about her early admission and departure with my family, there was excitement and encouragement. Pure celebration of this normal rite of passage. No hand-wringing about her being "too young" or concerns about her leaving home. The response was unanimous pride: "Of course she's ready. Look at how well you've prepared her."

The collision came in realizing that my American community was grieving what my Nigerian family was celebrating. American culture celebrates everything about launching kids except the mothers doing the launching. We get flowers on graduation day, then disappear into irrelevance. We're expected to smile through our own obsolescence and call it love.

But college? That's a playground with no benches for watching mothers. No zones for hovering. No way to step in when they fall. In most of the world, mothers don't become less important as children age, they become more important. But here, we've created a system where successful parenting means successfully eliminating our own necessity.

What they don't tell you is that drop-off day is actually your own graduation, from hands-on mothering to long-distance faith.

So, what do you do when you can't be there? You cover them, even when you can't reach them. I pray God covers them on the highways and the byways, the airways and, especially, the sideways. The places they shouldn't be. The places they go when they think we aren't watching. Whether you share my faith in this covering by God or find comfort in your own protective thoughts and energy, we all need something to hold onto when our arms can't reach.

I ask God to pluck them out before it goes too far. To arrest their hearts with peace. To flood their dorm room with grace.

I've spent more time on my knees since my children left than I ever did when they lived under my roof. There's something about distance that drops you to prayer like nothing else. When you can't text, call, or drive over. When all human methods of mothering are too slow, too far, or too limited, you learn to access the unlimited. And still, God whispers: "I've got them. My eyes are on the sparrow, how much more them?" You might find that assurance through your own quiet knowing or deep intuition, but for me, it's this personal God who sees every sparrow, and my child.

Faith after drop-off becomes less about believing in their safety and more about believing in their strength.

The Surrender That Sets You Both Free

Some days that belief comes easy. Other days, belief feels like an uphill climb. Those are the days when surrender feels less like release and more like restraint. Not just letting go, but actively holding back. Keeping my opinions tucked away. My warnings unspoken. My solutions offered only if directly requested.

So, I surrender. Not once. Not twice. But daily.

When the phone is silent. When the text is short. When the social media post doesn't sit right. When I have the urge to book a flight, show up, fix it. I surrender. Because love without control is still love. And motherhood without proximity is still motherhood.

Surrender teaches you this: it's not about giving up, it's about growing up. Both of you.

But here's the plot twist nobody mentions: The same skills that made us phenomenal mothers - adaptability, resilience, unconditional love, crisis management - are exactly what we need to reinvent ourselves. We didn't just raise future adults. We accidentally became them. While we were busy equipping them for life, we were quietly preparing ourselves for our third act.

There's a part of surrender that isn't loud or dramatic. It's the part that happens on a Tuesday, when you pass their empty room and straighten a corner of the bed that no one's slept in for weeks. It's when you buy their favorite snack out of habit, then catch yourself mid-reach, hand hovering in front of the pantry.

The grief isn't just about the big moments. It's about the thousand small routines that suddenly have no purpose. It's when a holiday approaches, and you begin to plan around absence.

The first Thanksgiving after my daughter left was a masterclass in surrender. This wasn't the clean grief of college distance, this was the particular agony of proximity without access. I set the table for one less because she was spending that day at her dad's house, forty five minutes away. She was home but not home with *me*. The cruelest mathematics of divorce is that your child can be in the same state and still be unreachable.

I declined my siblings' invitation, choosing the hollow echo of our empty house over the warm chaos of extended family. I couldn't bear to explain the absence, couldn't stomach the well-meaning questions about why she wasn't with me. Instead, I sat with the ghost of every Thanksgiving we'd shared.

I checked my phone too often. Jumped when it pinged. Smiled at the obligatory holiday text and group photo she sent, even as I ached for more. We created new traditions that year, smaller, quieter, different. Not better or worse, just... adjusted. Like pants hemmed after weight loss. They still fit, but they hold you differently. Surrender is not just a mother's grief, it's a family shifting its center of gravity.

I often think about how we keep looking ahead for the next thing, the next visit, the next phone call, the next moment of closeness, thinking it will satisfy the ache. But sometimes healing doesn't come in the next. Sometimes it comes in the now. Now, when the silence feels loud. Now, when the ache wraps around your ribcage. Now, when surrender looks like keeping your hands open even when you want to hold tight.

Waiting for their next visit home can become its own prison.

The Magnetic Pull of Shared Experience

The universe has a way of magnetizing people with similar interests or issues together, and suddenly I found myself in conversations I never expected to have.

It started with running into other parents in the community, casual encounters at the grocery store, the post office, church, that began with standard pleasantries but evolved into something deeper. Some conversations were canned, as easy and expected as "How are you?" "Fine." But others became surprisingly candid, and we'd find ourselves talking longer than was socially required, neither of us willing to break the connection that came from recognition.

It seemed almost every conversation I had during those first months led to the same announcement: "My daughter left for college. I'm an empty nester now." As if I had to declare it, to make it real by speaking it aloud, to find someone who understood this particular displacement.

What struck me was how differently we each carried this transition. Some mothers wore their empty nest like a badge of honor, "Finally! Time for me!" Others carried it like a secret shame, as if admitting they missed their children reflected poorly on their preparation for this moment. Still others seemed genuinely bewildered, walking through their days with the shell-shocked expression of people who'd survived something they hadn't seen coming.

But in those candid conversations, a pattern emerged. Whether we were celebrating or grieving, proud or bewildered, we were all asking the same fundamental question: "Now what?"

The mothers who seemed most at peace weren't necessarily the ones who'd prepared better or loved less, they were the ones who'd maintained some thread of individual identity throughout the intensive parenting years. They had hobbies that predated children, friendships that existed independent of school communities, interests that belonged to them alone. The rest of us were starting from scratch, learning to be ourselves again after decades of being someone's mother first and foremost.

The Revolutionary Act of Self-Nurturing

You see, surrender is not about weakness. It's about trust. Trust that the child you raised is growing into the adult they're meant to be. Trust that your prayers traveled further than your words ever could. Trust that what you see on the outside is only a fraction of the story God is writing. But it's also about something more revolutionary. Trusting that your story didn't end when theirs began somewhere else.

This realization came gradually, through those Tuesday morning meetings. Through conversations with other mothers navigating similar transitions. Through the quiet moments when I caught glimpses of who I was becoming. We've been conditioned to believe that good mothers disappear when their children no longer need daily care. That our value expires when theirs begins. That self-investment after motherhood is somehow selfish or inappropriate.

But what if this conditioning was never about producing better mothers? What if it was about producing women who wouldn't question their own dismissal from relevance? What if the message that we should gracefully step aside was less about family health and more about maintaining systems that benefit from women's unpaid labor and unquestioned sacrifice?

The more women I met who were reclaiming their lives after intensive motherhood, the more I realized this wasn't personal failure. It was a systematic design. A culture that teaches women to find complete fulfillment in service to others has created a massive population of skilled, experienced women who've been convinced they have nothing valuable to offer once that particular service ends.

So, I go back to the mirror. I remind myself I am still a mother. Still needed. Still powerful. Still loved. But more than that, I remind myself that my worth was never solely contained in the bins I packed or the frequency of calls I received. My worth is steady, anchored not just in the invisible cords of love that time and distance cannot fray, but in the woman I was before motherhood and the woman I'm becoming beyond it.

Learning to mother yourself is the graduation gift you never knew you needed. This, too, is a holy season. Not one I chose, but one I am learning to honor. Because letting go doesn't mean you stop showing up. It just means you show up differently.

Quieter. Wiser. Kinder to yourself.

I've learned that my own transformation doesn't stop just because the mothering changes. We're not done yet. We're just beginning again. With different tools. With deeper roots. With decades of wisdom and life experience that the world desperately needs, if we're brave enough to believe we still have something valuable to contribute.

And maybe that's the truly revolutionary act of reclamation. Refusing to believe that our most productive, creative, powerful years end when our children begin their independent lives. Instead, understanding that we've been in training for this moment all along. The skills we developed, the resilience we built, the wisdom we earned; none of it was just for them. It was also for us. For this season, for the contribution we're meant to make to the world now that our hands are free and our hearts are expanded.

To nurture our needs. To hold space for our dreams. To dust off the books we said we'd write, the languages we said we'd learn, the roads we said we'd take. To give ourselves permission to desire again.

This permission doesn't come naturally after decades of deferring our own wants in service of others' needs. It requires practice and intentionality. The same kind of daily commitment we once brought to raising children. But gradually, we must remember that having desires isn't selfish, it's human. That pursuing interests isn't self-indulgent, it's self-care. That

85

investing in our own growth isn't taking away from others, it's modeling what lifelong learning and personal development look like.

Through my photography, through the Tuesday morning coffee group, the Rising Tide community, through the simple act of saying yes to opportunities that served no one but myself, I began to rebuild a relationship with my own preferences. What did I actually enjoy? What energized rather than drained me? What made me feel alive in ways that had nothing to do with anyone else's approval or needs?

The answers surprised me. I discovered I loved the technical challenge of mastering camera settings in difficult lighting. I enjoyed the problem-solving aspect of composition and timing. I was energized by the interaction with clients who trusted me to capture their most important moments. I felt alive when I was creating something beautiful that would outlast the moment it was captured.

Beyond photography, other interests began surfacing. Solo travel became another unexpected rediscovery. I found myself energized by airports. By anticipation of packing and unpacking suitcases, by collecting entry and exit stamps at foreign destinations. Those colorful security stickers affixed to passports became small trophies of courage. Proof that I could navigate the world on my own terms. What mesmerized me most was meeting people across cultures and realizing that despite different languages and customs, we all want the same fundamental things - to love and be loved, to matter, to find meaning. Each journey became a way of experiencing the beauty of God's creation while discovering pieces of myself I'd forgotten existed.

None of this diminished my love for my children or my pride in their accomplishments. But it gave me a foundation of selfhood that didn't depend on their proximity or their need for me. It created space for me to celebrate their independence without feeling erased by it.

The Small Steps Back to Yourself

The first steps back to myself weren't dramatic, they were a daze of going to work and coming home. Lost in having all that time to myself. I found myself staring at hours that had previously been filled with someone else's schedule, someone else's needs, someone else's timeline. It was then I became more active in a small business and creative group called Rising Tide Society, a community I'd barely had time to engage with during the intensive mothering years. I gravitated toward the evening sessions, suddenly free from the dinner prep and homework supervision that had anchored my evenings for nearly two decades.

Meeting more women became my first revolutionary act. I had time to fill, not just the practical hours, but the emotional space that Charlie's presence had occupied. I poured myself into my photography, no longer shooting in stolen moments between carpools and practices, but with the luxury of unhurried attention.

Learning more about photography became learning to see differently. When I wasn't rushing to pick someone up or checking my watch against someone else's schedule, I could linger with light and shadow. I could wait for the perfect moment instead of capturing whatever was available in the narrow window between obligations.

I invested more in photography classes, some local, others that required travel I couldn't have managed before. I ventured into wedding photography, accepting second-shooter positions for other photographers. Suddenly, my Saturdays were free. No more band competitions commanding my weekends, I could commit to capturing other people's joy from dawn to midnight without consulting anyone else's calendar.

This wasn't just about photography. It was about discovering that my interests, when given space to grow, could flourish in ways I'd never imagined. The creative eye I'd developed while documenting my children's lives could serve a larger purpose. The patience I'd learned through years of waiting in car lines could translate into the stillness required for perfect shots. The organizational skills honed through managing family logistics could build a small business around something I loved.

Each Rising Tide Society meeting, each photography workshop, each wedding where I captured love in its rawest form, was a small rebellion against the voice that whispered I was too old, too late, too irrelevant to start something new.

It felt strange at first, guilty even. But the more I leaned into this self-nurturing, the more I realized: this wasn't selfish. This was stewardship. Taking care of the woman God had created, not just the mother I had become. The woman with dreams still unborn. With gifts still untapped. With a voice still waiting to be fully expressed.

The woman who had been patient enough to wait her turn.

If you ever doubt the power of surrender, let me tell you this: I've watched it transform the ache into purpose. I've seen it turn absence into space, for you to fill with what's next, with what matters, with who you're evolving into.

The Launch That Launches You Both

Standing in that Houston apartment after another airport goodbye, I finally understood what transformation really looks like: It doesn't happen in a single moment of revelation. It unfolds through a thousand small choices to reclaim what you've set aside. But first, I had to recognize the stranger in my mirror.

***

6

I Forgot Who I Was (And How to Remember)

"So is my word that goes out from my mouth: It will not return to me empty, but will accomplish what I desire and achieve the purpose for which I sent it."— Isaiah 55:11 (KJV)

***

The question came out of nowhere, posed by a stranger in the grocery store checkout line who'd noticed my empty cart and wedding ring.

"Just you today?" she asked with the casual friendliness of someone making small talk.

I opened my mouth to answer and realized I had no idea what to say. Yes, it was just me. But when had "just me" become so unfamiliar? When had I stopped being enough company for myself?

Standing there with my single-serving everything - one banana, one yogurt, one frozen dinner - I realized I'd forgotten how to shop for just me. More than that, I'd forgotten who "just me" even was.

The Beautiful Disappearing Act

Losing yourself in motherhood doesn't happen overnight. It's a slow fade, so gradual you don't notice until you're standing in a mirror wondering who's looking back.

I forgot what I liked to eat if no one else had an opinion. Standing in grocery aisles, I'd realize I couldn't remember my own preferences. Did I like strawberry or grape jelly? What was my favorite cereal when I wasn't buying what they would actually consume?

I forgot what music made me want to dance in the kitchen like nobody was watching. My playlists had become their playlists, my radio stations programmed to avoid the battles over car music.

I forgot the sound of my own voice when it wasn't responding to "Mom, where's my..." or "Can you sign this?" or "What's for dinner?" I'd lost the rhythm of my own thoughts, the cadence of conversations that weren't about logistics or their emotional needs.

Sitting in quiet moments like these, I started wondering: How many women were experiencing this same forgetting? How many had realized they'd spent so many years curating experiences for others that they'd forgotten what brought them joy? I started seeing the pattern everywhere. Women who'd become so fluent in everyone else's language that they'd forgotten how to speak their own. This wasn't personal failure. This was what happens when you love so completely that you forget to include yourself in that love.

Motherhood erases us, one forgotten preference at a time.

The most devastating part? This erasure feels like virtue. Society applauds mothers who sacrifice everything for their children. We're celebrated for our selflessness, our ability to put everyone else first, our talent for making ourselves invisible so our families can shine.

Somewhere in the beautiful work of raising them, I forgot I was also someone worth raising.

The Cultural Weight of Sacrifice

For African women, this erasure carries an extra weight that's rarely acknowledged. We're raised in traditions that teach us to be the backbone, the nurturer, the one who holds everyone together. Our mothers and grandmothers showed us love through service, identity through sacrifice.

I grew up watching women who poured themselves out like water until there was nothing left for their own thirst. Who worked double shifts to put children through school, who deferred their own dreams so someone else could reach theirs, who measured success by how little they needed for themselves.

This cultural conditioning made the disappearing act feel not just natural, but righteous. Every time I chose their needs over mine, I was following a blueprint written by generations of strong women who believed that self-sacrifice was the highest form of love.

But nobody had warned me what would happen when the people I'd sacrificed myself for no longer needed the sacrifice.

We learn early that our worth is measured by how well we disappear into the needs of others.

I became an expert at making myself small so they could be large. At blending into backgrounds so they could shine in foregrounds. At being forgettable so they could be unforgettable.

The contradiction of American motherhood hit me like a slap: We're supposed to raise independent children while remaining completely dependent on being needed. We're told to foster their autonomy while secretly building our entire identity around their dependence on us.

And then one day, you succeed. They don't need you anymore. And you realize you've spent so long being indispensable to them that you never learned to be essential to yourself.

When Your Own Child Sees the Emptiness

The first crack in my carefully constructed illusion came from the most unexpected source: my daughter herself.

As her departure for college approached, Charlie began asking questions that should have been simple but felt impossibly complex.

"Mom, what are you going to do when I leave?" she asked one evening while we were packing boxes for her dorm room. She was only seventeen, heading to college early, but her wisdom seemed far beyond her years.

I smiled and gave her the standard deflection: "Oh, I'll be fine. I'll finally have time to relax."

But she pressed on with the persistence of someone who genuinely cared. "No, really. What will you do? Maybe get a dog?"

The suggestion hit me with unexpected sadness. What she didn't realize was that her sweet attempt to help was just another form of caregiving, another life depending on me when what I needed was to learn how to depend on myself.

"You could take a foreign language course," she continued. "Or go back to school for your PhD, you've got your master's already. Maybe some certificate courses for your career?"

Each suggestion landed like a small indictment. She was seventeen years old, and she could see what I couldn't: that my life had been so completely absorbed into hers that without her, there was just... work and church.

"You could try salsa dancing," she added with a smile. "Remember how you always said you wanted to learn?"

I did remember. Vaguely. Like recalling a dream from years ago, the woman who once wanted to learn salsa, who once had dreams that belonged only to her. When was the last time I'd expressed a desire that had nothing to do with my children's happiness or success?

That conversation haunted me for weeks. Not because Charlie was being unkind, she was trying to help her mother imagine a life beyond motherhood. But because her questions revealed a truth I wasn't ready to face: I had no idea who I was when I wasn't taking care of someone else.

The Friend Who Saw Through the Fog

It was Jeff who finally called me out.

We were having lunch at our usual spot, the photography club we'd started with coworkers having dissolved months earlier when my focus shifted entirely to Charlie's college preparation. Jeff had been patient with my distraction, understanding that senior year of high school is academically accelerated, demands a certain kind of maternal vigilance.

But that day, he looked at me across the table with the directness of someone who'd known me for fifteen years and asked the question that broke me open:

"Ronnie, what do you want to do?"

"What do you mean?"

"I mean for yourself. For your own life. What do you want to do?"

I opened my mouth to answer and realized I had nothing. Nothing. Work. Church. That was it. That was the sum total of my existence beyond motherhood.

"I..." I started, then stopped. What could I say? That I'd spent my evenings watching shows I didn't particularly like? That my weekends consisted of catching up on chores and wondering what she was doing at college?

Jeff watched my face go through this internal crisis with the patience of someone who'd seen it coming from miles away.

"What about your photography?" he asked gently. "Remember when we started that lunch photography club? You were getting really good at it."

Photography. Yes, I'd enjoyed that brief experiment with creativity during lunch breaks. But I'd let it fall by the wayside as Charlie's college preparation intensified, as her needs took precedence over my nascent interests.

"You should take a real class," Jeff continued. "There's that weekend workshop in Virginia Beach with that photographer you talked about. What's stopping you?"

Money. Time. The ingrained belief that spending on myself was somehow selfish. But I couldn't say any of that to Jeff, who'd never accepted my excuses for not investing in my own happiness.

The silence stretched between us, filled with everything I couldn't say about how I'd forgotten I was allowed to want things for myself.

The Gift That Broke Me Open

Two days later, Jeff appeared at my desk with an envelope.

"What's this?" I asked.

"Half the cost of that photography workshop," he said matter-of-factly. "Consider it an investment in getting my friend back."

I stared at the envelope, overwhelmed by emotions I couldn't name. This man, this friend who'd chosen to see value in me when I'd forgotten my own worth, was literally investing in my rediscovery.

"Jeff, I can't ..."

"You can and you will," he interrupted. "Because fifteen years of friendship has taught me that you're worth betting on, even when you don't believe it yourself."

That night, I sat with Jeff's gift in my hands and cried. Not just because of his generosity, but because of what his gesture revealed: I had become so invisible to myself that it took someone else's faith to remind me I was still there.

The money wasn't just for a photography class. It was proof that someone still saw me as a whole person, not just a mother in transition. Jeff's investment forced me to confront a devastating truth: I hadn't just lost myself in motherhood, I'd convinced myself I was worthless without it.

His faith became the mirror I needed to see my own value. Sometimes it takes another person's belief to remind us we're still worth believing in.

The Archaeology of Self

Rediscovering yourself after years of motherhood isn't like finding a lost object, it's like archaeological work. You dig through layers of who you became to uncover who you were, all while trying to imagine who you might still become.

I started with small excavations. I bought a book I wanted to read, not because it would make me a better mother or advance my career, but because the cover called to me. I sat in a coffee shop and read for pleasure, without checking my phone every five minutes or worrying about someone else's schedule.

I took that photography workshop Jeff had invested in, driving to Virginia Beach on a Saturday morning with nervous energy and rusty creative muscles. Standing in a room full of strangers who knew nothing about my children, nothing about my identity shift, nothing about my identity crisis, I was forced to introduce myself as something other than "Charlie's mom."

"I'm Ronnie," I said. "I'm learning to see the world through my own eyes again."

It was the first honest thing I'd said about myself in years.

That weekend, surrounded by cameras and creative people, something dormant began to stir. Not just the technical skills of photography, but the permission to have preferences again. To like or dislike things based on my own aesthetic sense. To create something that belonged entirely to me.

I photographed shadows and light, textures and emotions. For eight hours, I existed purely in the present moment, not managing anyone else's needs or solving anyone else's problems. Just being. Just seeing. Just creating.

It was revolutionary.

The Integration

What I discovered in my journey back to myself wasn't that I needed to choose between being a mother and being a woman. I discovered that the skills I'd developed in twenty-three years of motherhood weren't obstacles to overcome, they were superpowers to be redirected.

The patience I'd learned through sleepless nights with sick children became the patience I needed to learn new skills as an adult. The problem-solving abilities I'd honed through endless childhood crises became the creativity I brought to my own challenges. The capacity for unconditional love I'd stretched and strengthened through decades of practice could finally include myself in its embrace.

I didn't lose myself in motherhood. I learned to love so deeply that I forgot to include myself in that love.

I learned that in that mirror, the woman who had been patient enough to wait her turn was still there. She hadn't disappeared. She'd been practicing. Practicing patience, wisdom, unconditional love, crisis management, strategic thinking. What if forgetting myself hadn't been failure but preparation? What if all those skills I'd developed weren't obsolete but transferable? The culture might not have a roadmap for women like us, but that doesn't mean we can't draw our own.

The woman I was rediscovering wasn't a stranger after all. She was the integration of who I'd been before motherhood and who I'd become because of it. She carried the wisdom of years spent nurturing others, but now she was learning to nurture herself with the same devotion.

You spent decades making yourself indispensable to others. Now it's time to make yourself indispensable to yourself."

I started wearing lipstick again, not for anyone else, but because it made me feel alive. I created space in my home that was just for me, a corner by the window where I could think my own thoughts without interruption. I began saying no to things I used to say yes to out of guilt, and yes to things that stirred something in my soul.

I made peace with the mirror, understanding that the woman looking back at me wasn't just who I had been or even who I was now, but the woman I was evolving into.

She had lines around her eyes that told stories of laughter and worry. Silver strands threaded through her hair like timestamps of seasons passed.

But there was something in her eyes, my eyes, that was both familiar and new. A spark of recognition, of possibility. This woman in the mirror wasn't broken or lost. She was emerging. She was remembering. She was transforming.

Writing this book has taken me over five years. Not because it's particularly long, but because revisiting these memories is like picking scabs off painful wounds, ensuring that what I document is my authentic lived experience, not some polished version that makes me look better than I am. I'm not sharing this story because I've mastered anything or because I'm better than anyone walking this path. I'm sharing it because I wish someone had told me that motherhood unfolds in phases, and each phase will pass even when it feels impossible while you're living it.

The children you pour your whole heart into raising will grow up and leave. And then there's you, standing in the quiet aftermath, asking "What now? What next?"

This book exists to help you begin answering those questions. Not with perfect solutions, but with permission to start imperfectly. Permission to reclaim dreams you deferred for two decades. Permission to discover new aspects of yourself that could only emerge when you finally had space to grow again.

The photography I'd abandoned during the intensive mothering years wasn't gone, it was waiting. The travel dreams I'd filed under "someday" weren't dead, they were dormant. The woman who used to have opinions about books and music and art that had nothing to do with anyone else's preferences, she wasn't lost, she was just buried under years of beautiful, necessary service to others.

Transformation isn't about replacing who you were with someone completely different. It's about integrating every version of yourself into who you're still developing. The dreams you deferred aren't lost time, they're seeds that needed the right season to grow.

My remembering didn't happen overnight. It required a deliberate process of excavation and reclamation.

Here's what Monday morning could look like when you're ready to start:

Week 1: Recognition Sit with a notebook and write down three things: Who were you before children? What did you love that had nothing to do with anyone else? What made you feel alive? Don't edit yourself. Don't worry about whether it's practical. Just remember.

Week 2: Release Make a list of everything you've been carrying that doesn't belong to you anymore. Their schedules. Their friendships drama. Their career decisions. Write each one down, then cross it out. This isn't abandoning them. It's acknowledging they can carry their own weight now.

Week 3: Reclamation Pick one thing from your Week 1 list. Not the biggest dream, the smallest one. If you loved photography, don't plan a safari shoot. Take pictures of your coffee cup. If you wanted to travel, don't book Morocco. Drive to the next town over. If you loved reading novels, don't tackle War and Peace. Buy one paperback that has nothing to do with self-improvement.

Week 4: Renewal Ask for help. Tell one person what you're trying to reclaim. Not your children, they're building their own lives. Find your Jeff, the friend who sees value in investing in your growth when you can't see it yourself. Accept that investment, whether it's fifty dollars for a class or fifty minutes of conversation that reminds you who you are underneath all the roles you've played.

This isn't about dramatic reinvention. It's about steady reclamation of the woman who was always there, waiting for her turn to grow again. The woman who spent decades pouring herself out finally learning to pour back in.

Start where you are. Use what you have. Do what you can. Monday morning is as good a time as any to remember you're worth the effort.

The Beautiful Return

The forgetting hadn't been failure. It had been necessary, a season of pouring myself out so completely that others could grow. But the remembering? The remembering was revolutionary. It was the recognition that the woman who had been patient enough to wait her turn deserved the same care and attention she'd given to everyone else.

This journey back to myself taught me something profound: You don't have to choose between being a devoted mother and being a whole woman. The same heart that loved your children into independence is capable of loving yourself into wholeness.

The same hands that packed their lunches can learn to create art. The same mind that solved their problems can dream dreams that belong entirely to you. The same spirit that cheered their victories can celebrate your own transformation.

The Invitation Forward

If you're standing where I stood, in front of a mirror, wondering who's looking back, know this: You haven't disappeared. You've been patient. You've been waiting. You've been preparing.

The woman you're seeing isn't broken or lost. She's ready. Ready to remember who she was before she became so essential to everyone else. Ready to dream dreams that are hers alone. Ready to take up space not because someone else needs her to, but because she deserves to.

The Third Act isn't waiting for you to stumble upon it. It's waiting for you to claim it. To step into it with intention. To understand that the skills you developed in Act Two, the patience, the wisdom, the strength, the love, aren't obsolete now. They're your foundation for what comes next.

So look in that mirror again. Not with disappointment at who you used to be or anxiety about who you might become. Look with recognition of who you are right now: a woman who loved so deeply she forgot herself, and who is now ready to remember.

And if you're blessed to have a Jeff in your life, someone who sees your worth when you can't, listen to them. Let them invest in your growth. Because sometimes it takes another person's faith to remind us we're still worth betting on.

Your calling is waiting. The Third Act is waiting. And the woman you're evolving into? She's been worth the wait.

7

Faith Before Freedom

"Be strong and of a good courage; be not afraid, neither be thou dismayed: for the Lord thy God is with thee whithersoever thou goest."— Joshua 1:9 (KJV)

***

The ache starts before the suitcase comes out.

It begins when they casually mention their return flight. When they start gathering scattered belongings, phone charger from your kitchen counter, that sweatshirt they claimed from your closet, the book that somehow migrated to your coffee table during their visit home. You feel it in your chest first. That hollow pulling sensation that has no name because some experiences live beyond words, beyond the vocabulary of normal human emotion.

Then comes the countdown that every mother knows by heart. Three days. Two days. Tomorrow. And you catch yourself doing things you swore you wouldn't do anymore, making their favorite breakfast though they claim they're not hungry, suggesting one more movie even though you've both run out of shows to watch together, stretching conversations like taffy because you know what comes after the words stop.

The leaving. The ritual that never gets easier, no matter how many times you perform it. The goodbye that feels like a small death every single time, even when you're proud of the life they're returning to. Even when you know it's right. Even when you know it's exactly what you raised them to do.

Here's the truth about loving someone with your own life. Very goodbye is both victory and defeat. Victory because they're confident enough to leave. Defeat because you're never ready for them to go.

Let me tell you what no one explains when they hand you that newborn baby seventeen years ago. You don't just fall in love with this person. Your nervous system rewires itself around their heartbeat. Your body learns to regulate itself by their presence. Your brain chemistry literally changes to accommodate the constant low-level awareness of their needs, location, and safety.

And then one day, usually around age seventeen, everyone expects you to just... turn that off.

"Let them go," they say. "Trust the process," they say. "You raised them well," they say. As if two decades of biological programming can be overridden by good intentions and positive thinking.

Here's what every culture knows but rarely speaks: letting go is unnatural. We're biologically designed to protect, nurture, and hold close. The impulse to release goes against every instinct that kept our children alive when they were small and vulnerable and completely dependent on our vigilance.

Western culture tells us to launch them at eighteen and celebrate their independence. Eastern cultures emphasize family bonds and staying close. But show me a woman anywhere who doesn't want to see them more often than they visit. Show me any parent who doesn't feel that pull when the phone call ends too soon. Show me a mother who doesn't check her phone one more time before bed, hoping for a text that says "thinking of you."

This ache lives in mothers from Tokyo to Toronto, from small towns to big cities to rural areas all around the world. We're all learning the same lesson: letting go isn't a personal failing, it's a universal challenge that deserves community support, not silent suffering. You can't. Because that ache is written into the DNA of love itself.

The Cultural Collision in My Chest

My heritage whispered the old wisdom; children belong to the village, love transcends geography, a mother's heart knows no borders. In the traditions I inherited from my Nigerian roots, children don't "leave home", they expand it. Marriage means more family, not less. Grandchildren mean the circle widens, not that it breaks. There's no concept of "empty nest" because the nest is designed to grow, not empty. But here I was, American-made despite my African roots, watching Charlie fold clothes into a suitcase bound for California while I faced a Texas apartment that would echo with silence when she left.

The cultural collision felt like whiplash: my heart wanted to gather the tribe closer while my adopted country expected me to celebrate launching everyone away. My mother's voice, carried across decades and continents, whispered that good mothers keep their children close. My American friends insisted that good mothers let their children go.

I was caught between two definitions of love, two measures of success, two completely different blueprints for how this stage of life was supposed to work.

In Lagos, a woman my age would be surrounded by family, children, grandchildren, relatives who understood that wisdom grows with age and elders become more essential, not less, as years pass. Her power years would be filled immediately with the next generation's needs.

But in Houston, I was learning the particular loneliness of American independence. The expectation that I would not only survive my children's departure but celebrate it. That I would reinvent myself from scratch at fifty-something and pretend that this was always the plan.

The truth? Both traditions carried wisdom, and both carried blind spots. The challenge was learning to honor my heritage while embracing my reality. I had to bridge two worlds of motherhood without losing myself in the gap between them.

I remember a conversation from Charlie's high school years that became my template for everything that followed. She was only sixteen then, overwhelmed by the pressure of early college applications. She was experiencing the weight of being academically accelerated and the complexity of navigating friendships when you're younger than everyone in your grade.

She sat on my bed one evening after a particularly difficult day, still in her school uniform, shoulders curved inward like she was protecting something fragile in her chest.

"Sometimes I feel like I'm failing at everything," she said, voice small in the gathering darkness of my bedroom. Every instinct I'd developed over sixteen years of motherhood screamed at me to fix it, solve it, carry it for her. I wanted to call her teachers, rearrange her schedule, eliminate every source of stress from her path. I wanted to wrap her in the kind of protective love that would shield her from every disappointment, every challenge, every moment of uncertainty.

Instead, something deeper whispered: *Create space for her to find her own strength*. It was the hardest thing I'd ever done, sitting in that silence while my child was in pain, resisting the urge to rush in with solutions and reassurances and the promise that everything would be okay.

"What do you think you need right now?" I asked instead. Long silence. I could hear the air conditioning humming and sudden traffic from an otherwise quiet street outside. The ordinary sounds of life continuing while we sat in this moment that felt anything but ordinary. Then: "I think I need to know it's okay to not know."

That's when I learned that faith before freedom isn't about having answers, it's about trusting the foundation you built together will hold them when they can't hold themselves. The mother in me wanted to eliminate her uncertainty. The woman in me understood that uncertainty was where courage grew. The human in me recognized that my job wasn't to remove her struggles but to help her develop the muscles she'd need to navigate them.

That conversation became my template for several similar conversations that followed: How do you love someone without trying to control their outcomes? How do you offer support without removing their agency? How do you step back far enough for them to step forward into their own strength?

The Practice of Letting Go

Charlie's first week at Elon, when she was just seventeen, I called almost every day. Not because anything was wrong, but because the silence in my house felt like a physical presence. I'd found myself reaching for my phone at 3 PM, the time she used to get home from school, only to remember that she was three states away, probably in class, living a life that had nothing to do with me.

The second week, I called every other day. By the third week, I was down to twice a week. By the end of the month, we'd settled into a rhythm that felt sustainable for both of us.

But the learning curve was steep and painful. Every instinct told me to maintain the connection that had defined our relationship for her entire life. Every piece of wisdom I'd ever received about healthy parenting told me to step back and let her establish her independence.

The practice of letting go, I discovered, is exactly that, a practice. Daily. Sometimes hourly. Choosing to trust instead of control. Choosing to believe instead of worry. Choosing to release instead of grasp. And like any practice, it got easier with repetition. Not because the love diminished, but because the expression of love evolved.

The Airport Liturgy

I've said goodbye at airports in Houston, Baltimore, DC, Dulles and Los Angeles. Different cities, same ritual. Same ache expanding like a balloon someone keeps inflating until you're sure it will burst your ribs, flood your chest cavity and stop your heart entirely. The ritual is always the same, a liturgy of love performed in fluorescent-lit terminals with perfect strangers as witnesses to your private heartbreak.

First comes the coffee shop conversation, both of you pretending this is just another casual conversation when you both know it's the last one for months. You ask about her flight time, gate number, whether she has enough snacks for the journey. She shows you pictures on her phone from whatever life she's returning to. Friends you've never met. Places you've never seen. Inside jokes you'll never understand.

Then the announcement: "Now boarding all passengers for Flight 1247 to Los Angeles."

The hug always lasts longer than it should. I'm the one who won't let go first. She's gracious about it, this woman who was once small enough to carry, who now carries herself with confidence that takes my breath away. She lets me hold on just long enough to memorize the feeling of her arms around me. The scent of her hair that still smells like home but now also smells like the life she's building elsewhere.

"I love you, Charlie," I whisper into her hair, words that carry the weight of every night I sang her to sleep, every morning I made her breakfast, every time I watched her walk away and trusted she'd be okay. "Love you too, Mom," she says, steady where I waver, strong where I'm fragile.

Then comes the moment that haunts every parent: watching them walk toward security, wheeling that suitcase filled with pieces of the life they built without you. But here's the detail that burns forever, it's not the walking away that destroys you. It's that split second when they reach the security line and pause, hand on their boarding pass, and decide whether to look back. When they do turn around, you wave like you're drowning. Like their acknowledgment is the life preserver that will keep you afloat until the next visit. When they don't, you die a little because you know they're finally, truly okay without you, which is exactly what you raised them to be, but somehow still feels like rejection.

Either way, you stand there until they disappear completely behind the security checkpoint. Because leaving first feels like abandonment, even when staying feels like torture.

Every mother knows this choreography. The forced smile that masks seismic internal shifting. The "text me when you land" that really means "prove to me you arrived safely in this world where I can't protect you." The casual tone that camouflages the fact that your entire nervous system is recalibrating to function without them.

We perform this ritual with Academy Award-level acting because we understand something profound: our children need to see us as confident in their leaving as we were in their staying. They need to witness our faith in their ability to navigate the world without us, even when that faith feels like the most challenging acting job of our lives.

The Solo Drive Home

The walk to the parking garage is always the hardest part. Your footsteps echo differently - heavier, more isolated, like the sound loneliness makes when it's trying to find its rhythm. In the car, you catch your reflection in the rearview mirror, red-rimmed eyes, but not regretful ones. This is what success looks like in parenting, working yourself out of a job so completely and thoroughly that they no longer need you to navigate their daily challenges.

The highway stretches ahead like grief itself, endless and unavoidable. You drive slower than usual, as if taking time will delay the reality waiting at home. The house that will be quiet again. The kitchen without her coffee cup in the sink. The living room that won't echo with her laughter at shows you've never heard of. The absence that will fill every room like an unwelcome houseguest.

But something shifts on that drive home in ways you never anticipated. Something profound and unexpected and quietly revolutionary. You start to remember who you were before you became essential to someone else's daily survival.

The silence in the car isn't just absence, it's possibility. The empty passenger seat isn't just loss, it's space for whatever comes next. The quiet that once felt like death starts to feel like potential.

You remember that you used to love driving alone. You used to relish the time to think your own thoughts without interruption. You remember having opinions about music that weren't influenced by what they could tolerate. You remember being interested in conversations that didn't revolve around their schedules, their friends, their challenges.

This is what they don't teach in parenting classes: identity shift isn't a phase you get over. It's a season you learn to live in. A new way of loving that requires different muscles, different skills, different kinds of faith. It's also, if you let it be, the beginning of remembering that you were always more than just a mother. You were always a whole person who happened to be raising other people. And now, for the first time in decades, you have the space to rediscover what that wholeness looks like.

Faith in the Letting Go

The faith before freedom isn't the Sunday morning kind with neat prayers and clean answers and happy endings tied up with scripture-shaped bows. It's the 3 AM kind, raw, desperate, clinging to promises you can barely remember in the dark when worry wakes you up and you realize you have no idea what they're doing right now or whether they're safe or whether they remembered to eat something other than pizza for dinner.

It's faith that asks the impossible questions. How do you trust God with someone you love more than your own life? How do you have faith in a future you can't see for people whose choices you can't control?

Faith that your children will be safe in a world that seems increasingly dangerous, increasingly unstable, increasingly hostile to the values you tried to instill.

Faith that the foundation you spent two decades building, the character lessons, the spiritual truths, the practical wisdom, took root deeper than teenage rebellion ever reached. Deeper than peer pressure. Deeper than the cultural messages that contradict everything you taught them about what matters.

Faith that God's love for them exceeds even yours, a thought both profoundly comforting and slightly overwhelming. The idea that Someone loves your children even more fiercely than you do, even more protectively, even more unconditionally.

Faith that your worth as a person, as a woman, as a human being created in the image of God, isn't tied to their need for you. That you have value independent of your usefulness to them. That your story doesn't end when their dependence on you does.

Faith that love doesn't diminish with distance, it transforms. It becomes less about daily care and more about lasting blessing. Less about immediate need and more about eternal connection. Less about what you can do for them and more about who you are to them.

Each goodbye builds this spiritual muscle. Each successful letting go, each moment of choosing trust over control, each decision to step back so they can step forward strengthens the faith that freedom requires. Because here's the truth that cuts both ways: the same faith that releases your children to their lives is the faith that releases you to yours.

Faith That Reshapes Your World

Standing in my Houston apartment after Charlie left for another semester, I understood something that would change the trajectory of my entire life. The faith required to let go of my children was the same faith required to take hold of my own dreams again.

The prayer that covered her in California could also cover me in Texas. The God who would direct their paths could also direct mine. The future I trusted for them could also be trusted for me. The love that had sustained me through decades of motherhood could sustain me through whatever came next.

This wasn't about replacing my love for them with love for something else. This was about expanding my understanding of what love could do, where it could take me, how it could transform not just my relationship with them but my relationship with myself.

The Visits That Are Never Long Enough

They come home for holidays, weekends, breaks between semesters or jobs or life transitions. You prepare like dignitaries are visiting, clean house, stocked fridge, cleared schedules. You research restaurants they might enjoy, plan activities they might remember, create space for memories you'll carry long after they leave again.

You stock their favorite snacks, the ones they grew up eating but can't find in their new city. You make sure their room is exactly as they left it, even though you know they've outgrown that space and probably prefer the independence of their own apartment. You clear your calendar completely because every minute feels precious, every conversation irreplaceable.

And then they're here, and it's wonderful and normal and somehow both exactly what you expected and nothing like you planned. They sleep late because they're exhausted from finals or work stress or the simple effort of maintaining adult life. They check their phones because they have friends and obligations and responsibilities that exist entirely separate from you. They meet old high school friends for dinners that don't include you because they're nurturing relationships that predate your current relationship with them.

You don't mind. Not really. You're grateful for proximity. For their voice from the next room, for proof they still choose to come home even when home is no longer their primary residence. You're thankful for the casual conversations over morning coffee. The shared glances at family jokes no one else would understand. The comfortable silences that speak to years of being together.

But the visits are never long enough. Never. Even when they stay for weeks. Even when you run out of things to do together. Even when you start getting on each other's nerves the way family does when too many personalities occupy too little space for too long.

When they mention their return flight, when the suitcase moves from closet to bed, when they start doing that mental inventory of belongings that signals the end of the visit, the ache starts all over again.

You'd think you'd get used to it. You don't. Each goodbye carries the same weight, the same disorienting mixture of pride and loss. Because each goodbye is proof that you did your job so well they no longer need you to do it.

Words That Fail

There's no English word for this feeling. No phrase in any language I know that captures the exact texture of loving someone so much you ache from their absence even when you're proud of their presence elsewhere.

Portuguese has "saudade", a deep longing for something absent, but it doesn't quite fit. Welsh has "hiraeth", homesickness for a place that may not exist, but that's not it either. Even my mother's Yoruba has "ayun" for the ache of missing someone, "ife omo" for the fierce love of a mother, but none capture this specific experience: the bittersweet joy of loving someone into their own life while mourning your own displacement from their daily story.

Maybe there are no words because this feeling is too large for language. Too complex for vocabulary. Too universal and too personal to be contained in syllables and consonants.

But here's what we know without needing words for it: The goodbye that breaks your heart is proof you loved well. The ache when they leave is evidence of connection, not failure. The pain of missing them is testimony to the depth of bond you created, the security you provided, the love you gave so freely they could walk away confident it would still be there when they returned.

Every mother in human history has known this feeling. In cultures where children stay close physically, the letting go happens gradually, different tribes, separate lives, but the heart recognizes the same surrender. In cultures of dramatic independence, the release is sudden, college, jobs, lives spanning continents, but the courage required is exactly the same.

We are part of an ancient sisterhood of women who've stood in doorways, watching their children walk toward futures we helped create but can't control. We are inheritors of a tradition that spans continents and centuries: the sacred art of loving someone enough to let them go.

The Freedom Faith Makes Possible

This gritty, imperfect, moment-by-moment choice to trust changes everything. Not just how you parent, but how you live. Not just how you love your children, but how you love yourself. Not just how you face goodbyes, but how you embrace hellos.

It teaches you that love isn't possession but a blessing. That strength isn't control but surrender. That success isn't keeping people close but helping them soar into whatever life they're meant to live.

It transforms your relationship with uncertainty. Instead of fearing the unknown, you learn to trust it. Instead of trying to control outcomes, you focus on building foundations strong enough to withstand whatever outcomes emerge. Instead of demanding guarantees, you develop faith that can function without them.

Most importantly, it transforms your understanding of worth. You discover your value isn't determined by how much others need you, but by who you are - independent of roles, separate from service to others, worthy simply because you exist.

The trust that covers them in their choices extends to trusting yourself in yours. The courage that steps back so they can step forward is the same courage that steps into whatever God has planned for your next season.

The Space That Wasn't Empty

What you thought was emptiness turns out to be space. Room for new growth, discoveries, expressions of the woman you've always been beneath the beautiful, necessary, but ultimately temporary role of hands-on mother.

The silence becomes canvas for new voices, your thoughts, dreams, conversations with God that don't revolve around someone else's immediate needs, plans that belong entirely to you.

The time becomes investment opportunity, in relationships you'd neglected, learning you'd postponed, service you'd never had bandwidth for, creation you'd always said you'd get to "someday," rest you'd forgotten you needed.

The identity crisis becomes identity expansion. You don't lose who you were, you add to it. You become mother-plus. Woman-and. The person who raised children and also the person who exists beyond that singular achievement.

In Houston, I started to understand that the space Charlie left wasn't vacant, it was available. Available for dreams I'd deferred for two decades. Available for purposes I'd never imagined. Available for the woman I was always meant to become but had been too busy mothering to discover.

The faith that trusted God with her future could also trust God with mine. The prayers that covered her journey could also sanctify mine. The love that released her could also embrace me.

The Revolution of Release

The courage to turn toward home, even when home feels empty, knowing that emptiness is just another word for possibility waiting to be filled with purpose. The revolutionary truth: the same strength that releases your children into their purposes releases you into yours.

Standing in my Houston apartment after another airport goodbye, I understood something that changed everything: I wasn't just learning to parent from a distance. I was learning to live with purpose regardless of distance. To love without needing to control. To trust without requiring guarantees.

The woman who trusted God enough to let go of her children could trust God enough to take hold of her own calling. The heart that loved without needing to possess could love herself without needing to diminish. The faith that covered them could also cover her journey into whatever God had planned for the decades ahead.

This is what faith before freedom really means: the courage to believe that the same God who called you to motherhood is calling you to something beyond motherhood. That the woman who shaped their characters is ready to reshape her own story. That the love that launched them is strong enough to launch you too.

The goodbye isn't the end of your story together. It's the beginning of all the stories you'll each write separately, and the faith that they'll be beautiful, meaningful, worthy of the love that made them possible.

***

8

Praying from a Distance

"The Lord is far from the wicked but he hears the prayer of the righteous."— Proverbs 15:29 (KJV)

***

I used to know the exact sound of their breathing.

Every intake, every pause, every soft exhale in the darkness. I could distinguish between peaceful sleep and restless dreams, between the rhythm of wellness and the slight wheeze that meant a chest cold was coming. My hand on their forehead could detect a fever before any thermometer registered the first degree. My ear pressed to their bedroom door could differentiate between genuine slumber and the careful stillness of a child pretending to sleep past bedtime.

I used to pray over their beds with my palm resting on their small backs, feeling their heartbeat against my hand like a prayer answered before I'd even spoken the words. Those whispered petitions hovered in the darkness above sleeping forms, protection for tomorrow's playground, wisdom for next week's test, courage for the friendship struggle they'd confided at dinner, strength for the growing pains that would stretch them into the people they were meant to become.

There was something sacred about those moments. Something tangible in the quiet rhythm of their breathing, the warmth of their skin beneath my palm, the complete trust with which they surrendered to sleep under my watch. I felt like a guardian at the gates, a priestess in the holy space between heaven and their dreams.

In those years, prayer felt immediate, necessary, effective. I could see the results of my intercession in their peaceful faces, their steady breathing, their ability to rest knowing someone was watching over them. Prayer was tactile then, my hands on their bodies, my voice in their ears, my presence as proof that someone cared enough to stay awake while they slept.

But that season has passed.

Now, I pray from a distance that spans more than miles, it spans lifetimes, time zones, and the vast geography of independent adulthood.

Prayer Across Geography

The first time I tried to pray for Charlie after she moved fifteen hundred miles away to USC, I found myself standing in my bedroom at 11 PM Houston time, which meant 9 PM in California, which meant she was probably studying or out with friends or living a life that had nothing to do with my prayer schedule.

My prayer felt like it died halfway to heaven because the space felt too vast, too quiet, too absent. How do you pray protection over someone when you don't know what intersection they'll cross today? How do you ask for wisdom on their behalf when you're no longer privy to their daily struggles? How do you intercede for their peace when their storms happen in time zones where you're sleeping?

That night, grief disguised as confusion left me wondering if distance had severed more than physical proximity. Had it severed my ability to mother them spiritually? Was prayer through a screen and across state lines somehow less potent than the whispered petitions I used to breathe over their pillows?

The questions felt like accusations: What kind of mother can't even pray effectively for her own child? What kind of faith crumbles at the first test of geography? What kind of spiritual life depends on physical presence to function?

But here's what I discovered in those first desperate months of long-distance mothering: What I lost in proximity, I gained in perspective.

The Evolution of Intercession

When Charlie lived under my roof, my prayers were tactical. Immediate. Focused on the test tomorrow, the friend drama today, the driving lesson next week. Every urgent petition was wrapped around the twenty-four-hour news cycle of adolescent crisis and celebration.

"God, help her remember what she studied for Algebra." "Please let that mean girl leave her alone at lunch." "Give her confidence behind the wheel." "Help her forgive me for being too strict about curfew."

My prayers were as small and immediate as my view of her world. Distance changed everything.

Suddenly, I was praying with a long lens instead of a microscope. Instead of begging God to help her pass individual tests, I found myself praying for a love of learning that would last decades. Instead of asking for popularity, I pleaded for discernment in choosing friends who would call out her best self. Instead of focusing on her comfort, I began praying for character, the kind that emerges only through challenges I couldn't shield her from even if I tried.

Distance taught me to pray beyond the immediate crisis toward the eternal character. Beyond today's problem toward tomorrow's purpose. Beyond what I could see toward what God was building in her that I might never witness directly.

The prayers became bigger because the perspective became wider. When you can't micromanage the details, you learn to trust the Designer with the overall blueprint.

The Prayer That Shifted My Foundation

It was during one of those college years when parenthood from a distance became a masterclass in faith.

The calls and texts came at random hours, each one a reminder that her world was spinning three time zones away from my ability to help. Sometimes it was a text about being sick with no one to bring soup or check her temperature. Other times, dental emergencies that required decisions I couldn't help make, choosing treatments while sitting in a dorm room instead of my kitchen where we used to discuss everything.

There were academic pressures that kept her up late while I worried from states away, knowing she was struggling with coursework that had moved beyond my ability to help. The ordinary crises of young adulthood that used to be my domain to fix - roommate conflicts, financial stress, the particular loneliness that comes with being far from home during difficult seasons.

Each situation was a reminder that the mother who had once driven through ice storms to reach a sick child couldn't drive away distance itself. The woman who had solved problems with presence, with chicken soup and tissue runs and the simple comfort of being near, now had to learn an entirely different kind of mothering.

One particular week, everything seemed to hit at once. A dental filling had fallen out requiring emergency treatment. Money was tight, and she was trying to manage expenses I couldn't monitor or control. Each text revealed another layer of stress, another challenge that my physical presence couldn't address.

I stood in my Houston apartment reading messages that painted a picture of struggle I couldn't reach. Problems I couldn't solve. A daughter who needed comfort I couldn't provide in person. Every instinct I'd developed over two decades of motherhood screamed at me to DO something. GO somewhere.

FIX this. But there was nothing to do except feel the weight of every mile between us like stones in my chest.

And that's when I learned what praying from a distance really means. It's not prayer despite the distance. It's prayer because of it.

For several hours, while she navigated decisions I couldn't make for her and stress I couldn't absorb, I prayed harder than I'd ever prayed in my life. Not the polite bedtime blessings of childhood, but desperate, raw, specific intercession that came from places in my soul I didn't know existed.

I prayed for wisdom for her professors whose responses would affect her confidence. I prayed for competent dental care from professionals whose names I didn't know but whose decisions would impact her well-being. I prayed for her roommate to be a source of encouragement instead of additional stress. I prayed for strength to sustain her until answers came, for the presence of God to fill the space where I couldn't be.

Something miraculous happened in those hours of helpless prayer: I felt closer to her than I had in months. Not physically - the miles remained unchanged. But spiritually, we were knit together by petitions that crossed every boundary except the one that mattered most. We were both held by the same invisible hands, both covered by the same unfailing love, both cradled in the care of the One who neither slumbers nor sleeps.

When the crisis passed - dental work completed, budget stretched to cover needs - I realized something profound: I hadn't just been praying for her. I'd been participating in her journey in the most essential way possible.

Distance teaches you that prayer, whatever form it takes for you, was never about your proximity to your children. It was about your connection to something larger that transcends physical space.

When you can't be there to check their temperature, the universe somehow holds them. When you can't drive them to important appointments, divine love goes before them. When you can't offer immediate comfort during heartbreak, something greater than yourself collects every tear and whispers truths into wounded hearts with more tenderness than you could ever provide.

Whether you call this force God, the Universe, Higher Power, or simply Love itself, the principle remains: your children are held by something far more constant and comprehensive than your physical presence ever could be.

This realization changes how you pray.

Instead of praying from the assumption that your presence is required for their protection, you begin praying from the confidence that God's presence is sufficient. Instead of interceding from anxiety about all the ways you can't help, you petition from faith in the ways He can. Instead of begging God to be what you cannot be from far away, you thank Him for being what He has always been, closer than breathe, nearer than heartbeat, more constant than any earthly love.

Prayer becomes less about bridging the distance between you and them and more about connecting with the One who was never distant from either of you.

The Universal Distance

Every parent who has watched a child walk away, whether you're a single mother like me, a married couple, a divorced father navigating custody transitions, or grandparents watching from even greater distances, knows this ache. The sudden awareness that your sphere of direct influence has shrunk while your sphere of concern has expanded infinitely.

Mothers in Tokyo ache the same as mothers in Lagos, mothers in London, mothers in Los Angeles, mothers in São Paulo, mothers in Sydney. The geography changes but the heart language remains constant. That universal dialect of love learning to stretch across distance without breaking.

My African heritage taught me that children belong to the village, that love transcends geography, that a mother's heart recognizes no borders. But American culture had convinced me that good mothering required physical presence, that distance equaled disconnection, that letting go meant caring less.

The truth lies somewhere between these two worldviews: Love doesn't require proximity to be powerful. Care doesn't demand presence to be constant. Prayer doesn't need physical nearness to be potent.

Surrounded by other mothers navigating similar transitions, I discovered that distance prayer creates its own kind of intimacy. The mother who can't hover learns to cover. The parent who can't manage learns to trust. The heart that can't hold tight learns to hold sacred.

My prayers for Charlie and her brothers have evolved from tactical to strategic, from immediate to eternal, from protective to purposeful.

Instead of praying for good days, I pray for them to recognize God's goodness in difficult ones. Instead of asking God to remove obstacles, I pray for strength to navigate them with grace. Instead of begging for easy, I pray for faith strong enough to handle whatever story God is writing through their experiences.

I pray for their character more than their comfort. For their integrity more than their income. For their spiritual growth more than their social status. For their relationship with God more than their relationship with anyone else, including me.

This isn't because I love them less than when they lived under my roof. It's because I've learned the difference between loving someone close and loving someone free. The kind of love that trusts them to the One who loves them most perfectly, most eternally, most redemptively.

I'm learning that praying from a distance isn't about trying to bridge the gap between us through spiritual effort. It's about recognizing that God has already bridged every gap that matters. That the same divine love that surrounds me surrounds them. That the same omnipresent grace that sustained me in Texas is sustaining Charlie in California and her brothers wherever their lives take them.

My prayers don't travel from my location to theirs, they meet in the space where love transcends physical boundaries. Whether you envision this as a throne room, the quantum field, universal consciousness, or simply the eternal place where love exists beyond space and time, the principle remains the same.

This understanding transforms prayer, or meditation, positive intention, focused love, whatever spiritual practice resonates with you, from desperate long-distance pleading into confident spiritual participation. I'm not trying to send my love across miles to reach them. I'm joining my voice to the constant love that already encompasses them, adding my specific, mother-heart intentions to the eternal care that never ceases.

Romans 8:34 reminds us that Christ himself "is at the right hand of God and is also interceding for us." My children and I are both beneficiaries of an intercession that never stops, never sleeps, never grows weary or distant. My prayers for them join a conversation that began before they were born and will continue long after I'm gone.

As I've learned to pray from a distance with open hands instead of clenched fists, something unexpected has happened. The space that felt like loss has become room for deeper faith. The quiet that seemed empty has filled with a different kind of intimacy with God. Conversations less interrupted by immediate crises, prayers less driven by urgent anxiety.

In learning to trust Him more completely with my children, I've discovered He can be trusted more completely with me too. The faith muscles strengthened through long-distance parenting have supported me through my own challenges and transitions. The spiritual disciplines developed through distant intercession have enriched my personal relationship with God in ways that proximity parenting never could.

This is the sacred exchange of this season: as you release your children to God's care, you receive deeper access to that same care for yourself.

The woman who learns to pray powerfully from a distance discovers she can also pray effectively for her own future. The mother who trusts God with her children's daily safety learns to trust God with her own daily provision. The heart that releases control of their outcomes becomes free to embrace whatever outcomes God has planned for her own life.

Here's the beautiful evidence that this spiritual mothering creates something lasting. Now Charlie calls me to add people to her prayer list. "Mom, can you pray for my friend Sarah? She's going through a rough breakup."

"Will you pray for my professor? His wife is having surgery."

"Can you pray for my job interview next week?"

The prayers that once flowed one direction, from me to God on her behalf, now flow both ways. She's learned to see prayer as a resource, intercession as a gift, spiritual support as something valuable enough to request specifically.

The distance that I feared would diminish our spiritual connection has actually deepened it. She knows I can't fix her problems from across the country, but she also knows I can pray for them from across the universe. And somehow, that feels more powerful to both of us than anything I could have done with my physical presence.

The Faith That Bridges Every Distance

Perhaps the greatest gift of learning to pray from a distance is discovering that distance is an illusion when it comes to the things that matter most.

Love doesn't diminish with miles. Care doesn't decrease with geography. Prayer doesn't weaken with physical separation. Faith doesn't fade with time zones. God doesn't become less present because we're not in the same location as our children.

The realization that breaks your heart and heals it simultaneously is that you were never your children's ultimate protector anyway. You were always just the instrument through which the real Protector worked. The temporary vessel through which eternal Love flowed. The earthly representation of heavenly Care. It was God's protection, flowing through your hands and heart and presence, but originating from a source far more reliable than any earthly mother.

Mothers worldwide are discovering this same truth. We're learning that the faith required to release our children teaches us to release ourselves from the limiting belief that our only value lies in our usefulness to others.

As I've learned to trust God more completely with their lives, I find myself trusting Him more deeply with my own. As I release my children to His care, I experience fresh freedom to pursue His calling in this new chapter. As I pray for their growth, I discover He's still forming me too - not despite the distance but because of it.

There is a gift hidden within the challenge of praying from a distance. It reveals that the God who bridges the gap between us and our adult children is the same God who continues to parent us all, regardless of our age or stage. None of us ever outgrow the need for divine guidance, grace, and growth. The distance that seems to separate us actually unites us in deeper spiritual kinship as we each learn to walk with God on our unique paths.

Standing in my Houston apartment, looking at pictures of Charlie in California, I understand something that transforms everything: we are all children learning to trust the same Father. We are all works in progress being shaped by the same hands. We are all beloved, regardless of our location or our life stage.

The mother who learns to release her children to God's care discovers she herself has never left God's care. The woman who trusts divine love with her children's futures can trust that same love with her own. The heart that prays powerfully from a distance learns that she herself is never distant from the heart of God.

So I will keep praying from a distance. With open hands. With trusting heart. With the confidence that comes from knowing we are all held in the same divine embrace, my children, myself, and generations of praying parents before me.

Because the hardest part about loving your children isn't letting them go, it's learning that your love was always meant to follow them, not hold them.

The prayers I whispered over their sleeping forms twenty years ago are still working. The petitions I breathed into their childhood are still being answered in their adulthood. The intercession that began when they were too young to understand continues now that they're old enough to participate.

Distance doesn't diminish a mother's prayers, it purifies them. When you can't be there to fix everything, you learn to trust the One who can. And that kind of faith moves mountains, even from three thousand miles away.

The geography of spiritual connection isn't measured in miles but in love. And love, I've learned, recognizes no boundaries except the ones we create with our own limitations, whether we call this practice prayer, meditation, sending positive energy, or simply holding space for their highest good.

My children are covered. By prayers that span decades and cross continents. By intercession that began before they were born and will continue long after I'm gone. By love that learned to let go without letting up. In learning to pray them into their futures, I've discovered that God is also praying me into mine. The distance that seemed like separation has become the space where both of our stories continue to unfold, guided by the same faithful hands, surrounded by the same unfailing love.

The prayer never ends. It just learns to travel farther and trust deeper.

This spiritual mothering creates connection that transcends geography. We're building a network of women who understand that distance doesn't diminish love, it transforms it into something more powerful than proximity ever could.

And that, I've discovered, is enough.

***

9

The Third Act Is Calling

"For I know the thoughts that I think toward you, saith the Lord, thoughts of peace, and not of evil, to give you an expected end."— Jeremiah 29:11 (KJV)

***

The phone call that redirected my next path came from the most unexpected source: my daughter.

As Charlie's college graduation was nearing, when I thought I had finally figured out my Houston life, when I'd grown comfortable with my one-bedroom apartment and my Tuesday morning coffee shop tribe, my phone rang with a conversation that would reshape everything again.

"Mom," Charlie said, her voice carrying that particular tone children use when they're about to tell their parents something they need to hear but don't want to say. "I've been thinking." I braced myself. After a decade of parenting an academically accelerated child who thought faster than most adults, I'd learned that Charlie's thinking usually led to changes I wasn't prepared for.

"I've decided to build my life in California," she continued. "And honestly? I think you need to be near your parents right now, not organizing your life around mine. And Grandma and Grandpa aren't getting any younger."

The words hit me with unexpected force. Here I was, thinking I'd finally found my footing in Houston, and my twenty-something daughter was gently pointing out that I was still unconsciously organizing my geography around her choices, still defining myself in relation to her path rather than my own.

She wasn't rejecting me or pushing me away. She was setting us both free to build lives that made sense for who we were, who we were evolving into, not who we'd been. But the realization that I'd spent three years building a life that was still fundamentally about someone else left me sitting quietly in my Houston apartment, processing a truth I wasn't ready to face.

That night, I walked around my Houston apartment, the one-bedroom space that had taught me I could live in rooms sized for my actual needs instead of everyone else's, and felt something shift. Not sadness, not even nostalgia. Recognition mixed with apprehension. This phase was complete. Houston had done its job. It had shown me I could survive alone, thrive alone, even reinvent alone.

But Charlie was right. I wasn't chasing her anymore. I was ready to chase myself. The question was: did I have the courage to uproot my life yet again in my early fifties?

Moving back to Maryland would mean returning to the house I'd rented out when I left, a financial anchor that had provided security but also obligation. It would mean waiting for my tenant's lease to expire, staying with friends in the interim, navigating the logistics of reclaiming a life I intentionally left behind.

It would mean explaining to friends and family why I couldn't seem to stay put. Why the woman who'd finally achieved independence kept moving around like she still didn't know where she belonged.

Most challenging of all, it would mean admitting that three years of self-discovery in Houston had led me to the conclusion that I still wasn't sure who I was or where I fit.

Starting over in your early fifties means every choice comes with financial implications you didn't have to consider in your twenties.

Moving back to Maryland meant coordinating with my tenant. Covering the mortgage payments until I could move back in.

Managing the logistics of another cross-country move on a budget that required careful planning. It meant acknowledging that while I'd maintained my financial independence, that independence came with constraints that shaped every decision.

But those constraints didn't stop me from dreaming. They just taught me to dream differently. When I eventually started traveling again, those solo trips to Mexico, the Dominican Republic, Caribbean islands, Turks and Caicos, Canada, Nigeria, Ghana, South Africa, Paris, Dubai, Turkey, Thailand, Singapore, Bali, Ireland I learned to travel strategically in most, focused on experiences and people rather than luxury. Each trip was inspired by something specific: a documentary about Turkish history, a book about West African culture, the movie Crazy Rich Asians that made me curious about Singapore's food markets. Eat Pray Love called me to Bali's spiritual energy, while Bangkok's legendary street food scene became irresistible.

The Turkey trip was a tour group with about eight stops over thirteen days, traveling with other women, sharing costs, choosing adventure over comfort. I wasn't staying at five-star hotels or flying first class. I was eating street food, staying in modest accommodations, prioritizing connection over convenience.

"Home is wherever I am," I tell people when they ask about all the stamps in my passport. "But the world is wide, and there's still so much to learn."

Each journey is an opportunity to expand my horizons and be changed by the people and experiences I encounter. South Korea is calling next, specifically Jeju Island, Busan, and Seoul, inspired by my newfound love of K-dramas and curiosity about a culture that celebrates both tradition and innovation. Vietnam and Japan follow close behind. Depending on when you're reading this book, I may have already discovered what those destinations have to teach me about resilience, beauty, and the possibilities available to a woman brave enough to move through the world at her own pace.

The Courage to Keep Growing

Moving back to Maryland taught me that the Third Act doesn't require you to become someone completely different. It requires you to become someone completely yourself, but that process is messier and more uncertain than the inspirational articles suggest.

The woman I was before children wasn't gone, she'd been enriched by everything that came after. The mother I was during the intensive years wasn't obsolete, she'd evolved into something broader, deeper, more intentional. But integrating all these versions of myself while navigating the practical realities of life in my early fifties? That was the work nobody had prepared me for.

The Third Act is about integration, not replacement. It's about addition, not subtraction. But it's also about accepting that you might try several versions of yourself before you find one that fits.

In Maryland, I found myself co-caring for my aging parents with patience I'd learned from caring for teenagers. I approached new friendships with wisdom earned through decades of navigating complex relationships. I pursued writing with the discipline I'd developed managing multiple children's schedules and emotional needs simultaneously.

Every skill I'd thought was specific to motherhood turned out to be transferable to the art of living fully. But transferring those skills to new contexts while figuring out where I belonged geographically, professionally, and personally? That was the challenge that kept me awake some nights, wondering if I was brave or just restless.

The Women Who Understand

The women's coffee group I'd joined in Houston was full of women asking similar questions. Not the women featured in magazine articles about glamorous reinvention, but real women navigating real challenges with grace and uncertainty.

Sarah, whose divorce settlement required careful financial planning for every major decision. Maria, who was caring for aging parents while supporting adult children through their own transitions. Janet, who was building a new career after her industry downsized women her age out of opportunities.

We weren't taking expensive pottery classes or opening artisanal bakeries. We were figuring out how to honor multiple responsibilities while still pursuing growth, meaning, and joy. We were learning that the Third Act often involves juggling dreams with duty, possibility with practicality.

When I told them about Charlie's suggestion that I move back to Maryland, their reactions were immediate and honest.

"Do you feel called to go back?" Sarah asked. "Because if you do, trust that instinct. But if you're just running toward the next thing because this thing feels incomplete, maybe sit with the discomfort a little longer."

"What draws you there beyond family obligation?" Maria wanted to know. "Because obligation alone isn't enough to build a life on, but combined with purpose, it can be powerful."

"Are you moving toward something or away from something?" Janet asked. "Because one leads to growth and the other just leads to more moving."

These were conversations about discernment, the kind that happen when women get honest about the complexity of choices that come with age, experience, and responsibility.

The Truth About Starting Over

The morning I finally decided to move back to Maryland, I wasn't filled with excitement or certainty. I was filled with a quiet determination mixed with healthy apprehension.

Packing my Houston apartment felt like closing a chapter, but not like admitting defeat. Each box I sealed represented something I'd learned about myself, something I could carry forward into whatever came next.

I kept thinking about that professor at Charlie's freshman orientation, the one who'd warned us that "this transition" would hit differently than we expected. Maybe this identity shift isn't just about missing your children. Maybe it's about discovering that growth doesn't follow a linear path, that developing yourself is a process that continues throughout your life.

The day before I left Houston, I drove around the city one last time, not to memorize what I was leaving but to acknowledge what I was taking with me. The confidence I'd gained from living alone. The friendships I'd built with other women in transition. The knowledge that I could start over if I needed to, that I could create community wherever I landed.

I wasn't leaving because I'd failed at Houston. I was leaving because Houston had taught me what it needed to teach me, and it was time for the next lesson.

The Call That Reshapes

The Third Act holds a truth: it's not a single destination.

It's a series of purposeful choices, each one building on the wisdom of the last. It's about remaining fluid, adaptable, open to the unexpected invitations life offers, even when those invitations come from the children you thought you were supposed to be giving directions to.

The Third Act is about learning that strength isn't staying in one place, it's having the courage to keep moving toward who you're evolving into, even when you're not entirely sure who that is yet.

Charlie's wisdom about returning to my roots while she built her life in California wasn't just about geography. It was about understanding that sometimes you have to circle back to move forward. That growth isn't always about dramatic change but often about deeper integration of everything you've learned.

I'm writing this not as someone who just discovered these truths, but as someone who has been living them for a decade. This isn't a retrospective from someone who "figured it all out" - it's a real-time report from the field, proof that transformation doesn't end when you think you've found yourself. It just keeps getting more interesting, more nuanced, more accepting of uncertainty as a permanent condition rather than a problem to solve.

The Universal Invitation

This is the moment. This is the movement. This is your Third Act.

It doesn't matter if you're 45 or 65. If your nest emptied last month or last decade. If you've been preparing for this season or if it caught you completely off guard. If you have resources or you're making it work on a tight budget. If you have family support or you're navigating this alone.

The invitation is the same: to step fully into the woman you've been developing through every season that brought you here, while accepting that growth is a process, not a destination.

Maybe your Third Act looks like going back to school, like the woman I met at a conference. Maybe it's creating art, like the neighbor who transformed her basement. Maybe it's serving somewhere unexpected, like the former teacher I read about.

Maybe it's traveling frugally to places that feed your soul. Maybe it's moving closer to aging parents while pursuing dreams you've deferred. Maybe it's something completely different, something only you can envision because it's shaped by your specific combination of gifts, experiences, and constraints.

After ten years of living this, here's what I've learned: whatever your Third Act looks like, it starts with a single decision.

Across the globe, women are making this same decision. We're refusing to accept that our most valuable years are behind us. We're building a movement of women who understand that the Third Act isn't about graceful retirement from relevance, it's about stepping into our most important work.

The decision to stop waiting for certainty and start moving with faith. The decision to embrace the questions instead of demanding immediate answers. The decision to honor both your dreams and your responsibilities while understanding that integration takes time.

The Time That Is Now

So what's waiting for you? What conversation have you been having with yourself for years, decades even? "Someday I'll..." "I've always wanted to..." "I wonder what would happen if I..."

The time for someday is now, not because you have all the answers or unlimited resources, but because waiting for perfect conditions is another form of hiding. This isn't about perfection or having it all figured out. It's about beginning where you are, with what you have, in the circumstances you're actually living rather than the ones you wish you had.

Your Third Act isn't a consolation prize for getting older. It's not a participation trophy for surviving the intensive years of parenting. It's not a graceful exit from relevance. It's a conscious entrance into the fullness of who you've always been evolving into, messy, uncertain, limited by real constraints, but still growing, still dreaming, still worthy of investment and care.

The curtain is rising. The spotlight is yours. And the script? You're writing it as you go, one imperfect, authentic, courageously uncertain page at a time.

Because the most beautiful truth about the Third Act is this: there is no wrong way to live it. There is only your way. And your way, with all its detours, uncertainties, and practical limitations, is exactly what the world has been waiting to see.

The Third Act is calling. It's been calling for years, waiting patiently while you attended to everyone else's growth.

Now it's time to answer, not with certainty about where it will lead, but with faith that the journey itself is worthwhile.

***

10

For Every Daughter Who Will One Day Understand

"The Lord bless you and keep you; the Lord make his face shine on you and be gracious to you; the Lord turn his face toward you and give you peace." — *Numbers 6:24-26 (KJV)*

***

One day, when you stand where I stand now, you'll understand.

Not because someone explained it to you, but because life will teach you what words never could. You'll understand why I stood at your bedroom door long after you'd fallen asleep, just watching you breathe. Why I took pictures of ordinary Tuesday afternoons. Why I cried the first time you chose a friend's house over ours for a sleepover.

You'll understand that a mother's love is the only love in the world that aims for its own obsolescence and breaks its own heart in the process.

Charlie, my dearest daughter, this letter is for you and for every daughter who will one day face the sacred mystery of loving someone enough to let them go.

The Things I Couldn't Tell You Then

I wasn't prepared for how quickly time would move. How the days that felt endless, packed lunches, homework battles, bedtime stories that stretched into deep nighttime talks, would become memories faster than I could gather them. How I'd wish for quiet during the chaos, then ache for noise during the silence.

You'll understand the irony that haunts every mother: how desperately we sometimes wish away the very things we'll later long for.

But there were things happening in those ordinary moments that I couldn't tell you then because you wouldn't have understood. Things that were breaking my heart and healing it simultaneously. Things that were preparing both of us for the day when love would mean letting go.

The Bathroom Door Prophecy

I remember when you were small, maybe four or five, following me everywhere, even to the bathroom. Your little fingers would appear under the door, wiggling as if to reach for me, to maintain that connection even through a barrier.

"Mommy, what are you doing? Mommy, can I come in? Mommy, are you almost done?"

I'd sigh, sometimes with impatience, dreaming of the day when I could use the bathroom in peace.

And now? Now the house is so quiet I can hear the refrigerator humming from rooms away. Now I find myself standing outside closed doors, not to escape but to feel closer to memories of noise and chaos and the beautiful invasion of a child who couldn't bear to be separated from me even by a bathroom door.

One day, you'll understand that those little fingers under the door weren't an invasion of privacy, they were love made visible. The purest form of "I need you near me" your small heart knew how to express.

One day, when your own child follows you to the bathroom, when tiny fingers appear under your door reaching for connection, you'll remember this moment. And instead of sighing with impatience, you'll smile through tears, knowing that these invasions are temporary, precious, and heartbreakingly finite.

The Sneaker Store Heartbreak

You probably don't remember, but when you were about eight, you asked for those expensive sneakers all the kids at school were wearing. Not demanded, you were raised better than that, but asked with that careful politeness children use when they want something they suspect they can't have.

"Mom, could I maybe get those shoes? The ones with the lights that flash?"

I saw the hope in your eyes, the way you'd prepared yourself for disappointment but couldn't help wanting anyway. I saw how you'd noticed what the other kids wore, how you'd calculated that maybe, just maybe, this time would be different.

"Not this time, sweetheart," I said, my heart breaking as I watched your face carefully rearrange itself from hope to acceptance. "But we can look at some other options."

You nodded. Smiled. Said, "Okay, Mom. These are fine too," as we picked up the sensible shoes that would last but wouldn't light up, wouldn't make you feel special, wouldn't help you fit in with the children whose parents said yes to things mine couldn't.

What you didn't see was me going back to that store three times over the next week, standing in front of those shoes, calculating and recalculating our budget, wondering if I was teaching you the value of money or just teaching you that you couldn't have what you wanted.

What you didn't know was that I cried in the car that day, not because you'd thrown a fit or made me feel guilty, but because you hadn't. Because you'd accepted disappointment with such grace that it broke my heart. Because I was raising a child who understood sacrifice before she understood abundance.

One day, when your own child asks for something you can't afford, when you see that same careful hope in their eyes, you'll understand that saying no to what they want while saying yes to what they need is one of the hardest parts of loving someone well.

You'll understand that those moments weren't about shoes or sleepovers or things. They were about teaching you that love doesn't always look like getting what you want, that sometimes the deepest care comes wrapped in disappointment.

The Last Time You Needed Me

There was a last time for everything, and I missed most of them because I didn't know they were happening.

The last time you crawled into my bed after a nightmare. The last time you asked me to read you a bedtime story. The last time you needed help tying your shoes, brushing your teeth, reaching something from a high shelf.

The last time you said "Mommy, watch this!" before performing some small miracle of childhood, a cartwheel, a drawing, a song you'd learned.

I didn't know to memorize those moments. I didn't know to hold them longer, savor them more deeply, understand that ordinary Thursday afternoons can contain last times that will echo in your heart for decades.

But there's one last time I do remember, and it still takes my breath away.

You were maybe twelve or thirteen, struggling with a math problem that had reduced you to frustrated tears. You'd been working on it for an hour, eraser shavings scattered across the kitchen table like evidence of defeat.

"Mom," you said, your voice small and defeated, "can you help me?"

I sat down beside you, looked at the problem, and realized with a jolt that it was beyond my understanding. When had math become so complex? When had your homework outgrown my ability to help?

"Let's figure this out together," I said, pulling up an online tutorial on my laptop.

For the next hour, we learned together. You teaching me concepts that came naturally to your young mind, me helping you organize your thoughts into clear steps.

When you finally solved it, your face lit up with triumph. "Thanks, Mom. I think I understand it now."

What you didn't see was the bittersweet realization washing over me: this was probably the last time you'd need my help with homework like that. From now on, you'd be the teacher and I'd be the student, learning from the mind I'd helped shape but could no longer guide.

One day, you'll understand that every "last time" is also a "first time", the first time they're independent enough not to need you, the first glimpse of the adult they're evolving into.

And you'll understand that watching them outgrow your ability to help them is one of the most beautiful and heartbreaking successes of motherhood.

The Echo of Your Voice

Once, I overheard you talking to a friend who was crying about her parents' divorce. I wasn't eavesdropping, you were in the next room, and voices carry.

"I know it feels like everything is falling apart," you said, your voice gentle but steady. "But sometimes things have to fall apart so better things can come together. Your parents love you, that hasn't changed. How they show it might look different now, but the love is still there."

I stood frozen in my kitchen, tears streaming down my face, because those were my words. Not exactly, you'd made them your own, improved them even. But the heart of what you were saying, the way you were holding space for someone else's pain while offering hope, that was love I'd taught you, wisdom we'd built together through years of bedtime conversations and difficult questions.

You were mothering your friend with tools you'd learned from my own divorce, but using them in your own way, with your own wisdom added to mine.

In that moment, I understood something that took my breath away: the best parts of me would live on in you, but they'd be better because they'd be filtered through your experience, your perspective, your heart.

You weren't just my daughter anymore. You were my legacy, walking around in the world, spreading love and wisdom and comfort to people I'd never meet, in ways I'd never imagine.

One day, you'll hear your child say something that sounds like you, but better. You'll recognize your words coming from their mouth, but refined, improved, made more beautiful by their unique understanding.

And you'll realize that this is immortality, not living forever, but living on in the hearts and voices and wisdom of the people you've loved well.

The Last Bedtime Story

I don't remember the last time I read you a bedtime story, and that haunts me.

Was it "Goodnight Moon"? "Where the Wild Things Are"? Something from Junie B. Jones? Some chapter from a book we'd been reading together, night after night, until you were old enough to finish it yourself?

I don't remember because I thought there would always be another night, another story, another chance to lie beside you in the dark and share the magic of words creating worlds.

But there was a last time. A final bedtime story that I read without knowing it was the end of an era that had defined our relationship for years.

What I do remember is the night you said, "Thanks, Mom, but I think I'll just read to myself tonight." You said it so casually, as if you weren't ending one of the most sacred rituals of your childhood. As if you weren't gently closing the door on a tradition that had been my favorite part of every day.

I said, "Okay Jo. You were Jo then, calling you Charlie came much later," and kissed your forehead and turned off the light, not understanding that I was walking away from the last bedtime of your childhood.

After that, you read yourself to sleep. First picture books, then chapter books, then novels that took you to places I'd never been, taught you things I'd never learned.

I would walk past your room and see the glow of your reading light under the door, hear the soft whisper of pages turning, and feel proud and heartbroken in equal measure.

Proud because you'd become a reader, a lover of stories, someone who found comfort and adventure in books.

Heartbroken because my voice was no longer the last one you heard before sleep, my stories no longer the dreams that carried you through the night.

One day, your child will outgrow bedtime stories. They'll gently tell you they're old enough to read alone, and you'll say okay and kiss them goodnight, not realizing you're closing the book on one of the most precious chapters of motherhood.

When that happens, don't grieve too long. Instead, feel grateful for every story you shared, every night you spent creating magic with your voice and their imagination.

And remember that even though they don't need you to read to them anymore, you taught them to love stories. You gave them the gift of finding worlds between pages, of never being alone as long as there are books to read.

That's a kind of immortality too, your voice living on in their love of words, your stories echoing in every book they'll ever read.

The Night Your Name Became Ours

I need to tell you how "Charlie" was born, because someday when you're tucking your own children into bed, you'll understand the sacred power of a mother's voice calling their name.

Friday nights were the only school nights you could stay up late, a family tradition that made the end of each week feel like a small celebration. Jeffrey and Jason would sprawl across the living room, and you'd curl up with whatever book had captured your imagination that week.

When I'd finally head upstairs for bed, I'd call out my goodnights from the stairs: "Goodnight Jeffrey! Goodnight Jason!" Two syllables each, rolling off my tongue like a familiar song.

But when I got to you: "Goodnight JoAnna!" Three syllables. It felt clunky, formal, like I was calling to a stranger instead of my baby girl.

One Friday night, without thinking, "Goodnight Charlie!" popped out instead. Two syllables. It felt right immediately, like finding the perfect note in a melody I'd been trying to hum.

You called back, "Goodnight Mom!" but I could hear the smile in your voice, even from downstairs, or maybe it was my imagination.

From that night forward, you were Charlie to me. Not to the world, not to your teachers or friends, but to me. It became our thing, this name that belonged only to the space between us, a syllable of love that fit perfectly in my mouth and made you mine in a way that had nothing to do with birth certificates or formal introductions.

Years later, when I stood on cold asphalt calling "Charlie!" into the dawn air at a garbage truck, it wasn't just your name I was calling. It was seventeen years of Friday night goodnights, seventeen years of a love so specific it required its own language.

When you become a mother, you'll understand that some names aren't chosen, they're born from love that needs exactly the right sound to express itself.

The Day I Found Your List

I wasn't snooping. I was cleaning your room after you'd left for college, a futile attempt to keep busy, to feel useful, to maintain some connection to the space that had been yours for so many years.

Under your bed, tucked between old textbooks and forgotten school papers, I found a piece of paper in your handwriting. A list you'd made, probably during one of those teenage moments when everything felt overwhelming.

"Things I'm Grateful For," it said at the top.

Most of the items were what you'd expect: friends, family, your favorite foods. But three items on that list stopped my heart:

"Mom's terrible singing in the car" "The way Mom always has tissues in her purse" "How Mom never gave up on me during algebra"

I sat on your bedroom floor and sobbed.

Not because the list was particularly profound or beautifully written, but because it was evidence of something I'd never been sure of: that the small things mattered. That my off-key singing during car rides hadn't embarrassed you, it had comforted you.

Well, except when it was my turn to drive carpool, picking up your friends. You used to beg me before we arrived not to sing with your friends in the car, so I wouldn't embarrass you. "Please, Mom, just this once, can you not sing?" you'd whisper, your face flushed with that particular mortification only teenagers can feel.

But during our regular drives to school, just the two of us, those were different. We used to take sunrise photos on those drives, capturing the way the morning light painted the sky different colors each day. I still have those photos on my phone, hundreds of them, each one a memory of a moment when it was just us and the road and whatever song was playing.

Your list reminded me that being prepared with tissues and extra patience wasn't just mothering, it was love made visible in ways you noticed and treasured.

For years, I'd worried about the big things. Was I providing enough opportunities? Making the right educational choices? Preparing you adequately for the world?

But your list reminded me that love lives in the details. In terrible car singing and pocket tissues and sitting at the kitchen table night after night, explaining math concepts I barely understood myself, refusing to give up because you needed to know that I believed you could figure it out.

One day, you'll find evidence of your own impact in unexpected places. A drawing your child made of your family where you're smiling. A school essay where they write about you as their hero. A gratitude list that includes things you never knew they noticed.

When that happens, you'll understand that the small acts of love, the ones you do without thinking, the ones that feel ordinary and unremarkable, are often the ones that matter most.

You'll understand that love isn't just in the grand gestures, but in the tissue you hand them when they're crying, the song you sing even though you can't carry a tune, the way you never give up on them even when they want to give up on themselves.

The Gifts I Didn't Know I Was Giving

Every lullaby was a blessing. Every band-aid on a scraped knee was preparation for bigger wounds I couldn't heal. Every homework session was training for problems I couldn't solve for you.

But I didn't know it then. I thought I was just getting through the days, meeting immediate needs, hoping I wasn't messing up too badly.

I didn't know that teaching you to tie your shoes was also teaching you persistence. That reading bedtime stories was also building your capacity for imagination. That making you clean your room was also developing your ability to take care of yourself and your space.

I didn't know that every time I apologized when I was wrong, I was showing you that adults can admit mistakes and still maintain authority. That every time I kept a promise, I was building your capacity to trust. That every time I followed through on consequences, I was teaching you that actions have predictable outcomes.

I didn't know that the fights we had about curfew and chores and respect were actually practice for the bigger negotiations you'd have with bosses and roommates and romantic partners.

I didn't know that I wasn't just raising a child. I was raising my own replacement in your life.

This is what mothers don't tell daughters: we're not just nurturing children. We're nurturing our own obsolescence, day by day, choice by choice, love by love.

The Sacred Exchange

But here's the mystery I'm still learning: as I release you to your own life, I don't lose you. I find a different version of you. Not the child who needed me to tie her shoes and check her homework, but the woman who chooses to share her life with me because she wants to, not because she has to.

The daughter who calls not because she needs something, but because she has something to give.

The young woman who texts me articles she thinks I'd find interesting, who shares photos of her life not because I'm monitoring but because she wants me to see what brings her joy.

The exchange feels sacred; blessing your children forward: what looks like loss becomes transformation. What feels like ending becomes beginning. What seems like goodbye becomes a new kind of hello.

When you understand this, you'll know why I stopped trying to be the GPS for your life and learned to be the home base instead. Not the voice that tells you which direction to go, but the light that stays on so you can find your way back when you need to.

For the Mother You Will Become

When you choose motherhood, you'll understand the impossible mathematics of maternal love: how it multiplies with every breath they take and divides your heart with every step they take away from you.

You'll understand why I kept your baby clothes long after you outgrew them. Why I saved every Mother's Day card you made with construction paper and crooked letters. Why I took videos of you singing in the car and reading books aloud and having conversations with your stuffed animals.

You'll understand why I stood in your empty room that first night after you left for college and cried not because I was sad, but because I was proud and terrified and grateful all at once.

You'll understand that a mother's love doesn't diminish when her children leave, it transforms into something broader, deeper, more mature. Love that trusts instead of controls. Love that blesses instead of clings. Love that celebrates independence instead of mourning dependence.

You'll understand why I prayed for your happiness but didn't try to manufacture it. Why I wanted to give you everything but knew the most important things had to be earned. Why I taught you to be strong enough to stand without me, even though part of me wanted you to need me forever.

And you'll understand that every choice I made, even the wrong ones, especially the wrong ones, came from a love so vast it sometimes scared me.

The Understanding That Comes

When your own children test their wings, you'll remember standing at my bedroom door at 3 AM, wanting to wake me up just to tell me about a dream or share a midnight worry. You'll understand why I always said "Come in" even when I was exhausted, why I made time for conversations that seemed circular and questions that had no clear answers.

When you find yourself making the same mistakes I made, loving too fiercely, protecting too completely, worrying too much, you'll understand that I wasn't perfect, but I was present. I wasn't always right, but I was always rooting for you.

When you hold your own child for the first time, you'll finally understand the magnitude of the love I tried so hard to express but could never fully capture in words.

You'll understand why I took so many pictures that you complained about posing for. Why I wanted "just one more" when you were ready to be done with family photos. Why I insisted on documenting ordinary moments that seemed completely unremarkable to you.

You'll understand that I was trying to hold onto time that I knew was slipping away, trying to capture the essence of a childhood that I knew would be over too soon.

The Legacy of Letting Go

What I hope you'll understand most of all is this: The faith that releases your children teaches you to release yourself from limiting beliefs about your worth.

Every time I chose to step back instead of step in, I was giving you space to discover your own strength. Every time I bit my tongue instead of offering unsolicited advice, I was allowing you to develop your own wisdom. Every time I loved you enough to let you make your own mistakes, I was investing in the woman you would become.

This is the greatest gift one generation can give to the next: not protection from all storms, but faith that they can weather whatever comes.

When you were seventeen and wanted to go to college in Boston, every instinct told me to encourage you to stay closer to home. But I looked at your face when you talked about your dreams, and I knew that my job wasn't to make you feel safe, it was to make you feel capable.

When you wanted to transfer to USC as a sophomore, when you decided to stay in California after graduation, when you chose paths I wouldn't have chosen for you, every time, I had to choose between my need for proximity and your need for autonomy.

I chose you. Every time, I chose what would help you become who you were meant to be, even when it meant letting go of who I needed you to be for my own comfort.

The Promise That Remains

Even in the letting go, we remain connected by invisible threads of shared history, genetic legacy, and love that defies simple definition.

I may not be the first person you call with good news anymore, but I'm still the one who taught you to celebrate.

I may not be your primary source of comfort during hard times, but I'm still the one who showed you that comfort exists.

I may not be your main advisor for life decisions, but I'm still the one who taught you to trust your own judgment.

I may not be the center of your universe anymore, but I'll always be part of your constellation, one of the fixed stars you can navigate by when everything else feels uncertain.

The oak tree doesn't mourn the acorns that fall from its branches. It celebrates them. Each acorn carries the full potential of the tree that released it, plus the possibility of growing into something even greater. The oak knows that its greatest legacy isn't in its own height or beauty, but in the forests that grow from what it has the courage to let go.

So it is with us.

The Circle That Never Breaks

One day, you'll understand that our connection was never about proximity. It was about something invisible and unbreakable, the spiritual DNA that links us across any distance, through any season, beyond any circumstance.

This understanding connects you to millions of daughters who will one day stand where I stand now. You'll join the ancient sisterhood of women who've learned that the greatest gift we can give our children isn't our continued sacrifice, but our example of what it looks like to keep growing.

You'll understand that I'm not just your mother. I'm your first teacher in the art of love, your first example of what it means to give without counting the cost, your first glimpse of what unconditional means.

And you'll understand that the love I've given you, imperfect as it was, has created roots deep enough to sustain you through every season of separation and return.

When you become a mother yourself, you'll join this timeless community of women who've loved children into independence, who've blessed them forward even when it broke their hearts, who've discovered that the love that lets go is the love that lasts forever.

This sisterhood spans continents and generations. We're building something beautiful together, a network of mothers who refuse to disappear when our children launch. We're proving that the women who raised the future deserve to help shape it.

And you'll understand that our story isn't ending. It's beginning again, in you.

The Final Blessing

One day, you'll understand that this was never about me keeping you. It was about me giving you everything you needed to keep yourself.

One day, you'll understand that the hardest job in the world isn't raising children, it's raising children who don't need you to raise them anymore.

One day, you'll understand that the greatest success of my motherhood wasn't in how much you needed me, but in how little you need me now to be exactly who you were created to be.

But today, just know this: You were, and always will be, my greatest transformation.

The child who taught me what love without limits looks like. The daughter who showed me what faith in action means. The woman who proved that the best gift you can give someone you love is the freedom to become themselves.

So I bless you forward, my daughter. Into the hands of the One who knew you before I did, who loves you more perfectly than I ever could, whose plans for you exceed even my wildest dreams for your life.

I bless the path you're walking, even when it leads away from mine.

I bless the choices you're making, even when they're different from the ones I would make.

I bless the woman you're evolving into, even though she's outgrowing the need for who I've been to her.

I bless your independence without mourning my obsolescence.

I bless your strength without taking credit for it.

I bless your future without needing to direct it.

And I bless the mystery of maternal love that somehow grows stronger through letting go, deeper through distance, more complete through release.

When you finally understand all of this, really understand it in your bones and heart and soul, you'll know that our story isn't ending.

It's beginning again, in you.

With all my love and faith in your next transformation,

Mom

P.S. Keep the tissues handy for when you become a mother yourself. You'll need them for all the moments when love breaks your heart open in the most beautiful way possible.

***

11

Things I Wish I Told You

*"Let your speech be always with grace, seasoned with salt, that
ye may know how ye ought to answer every man."*
— Colossians 4:6 (KJV)

***

There are conversations that live in the space between what we
say and what we mean. Words that get swallowed by pride, buried
by fear, or simply lost in the ordinary rush of days that felt endless
until they were over.

These are the things I wish I'd said, Charlie. Not because you
needed to hear them then, but because saying them now might
help some other mother find her voice when it matters most.

I wish I told you that I was scared too.

I played it cool, didn't I?

I gave you the speech. The hugs. The cash. The checklist.

I told you how proud I was, how much faith I had in your
future. And I meant every word.

But what I didn't say was, I was scared too.

Not of who you would become. Not of you failing.

I was scared of the silence that would follow. Of the dinner
table with one less chair. Of walking past your room and hearing
... nothing.

I didn't tell you that I stood in the store staring at laundry
detergent and had to blink back tears because I remembered how

picky you were about the scent. How you'd sniff every bottle like a sommelier before declaring which one was "acceptable."

I didn't tell you that I rehearse our conversations in my head before I text you, editing and re-editing messages to strike the perfect balance between caring and clingy.

I didn't tell you that I whisper prayers over you in the morning and again at night, and again if I see your status say "active now" at 2 a.m., wondering what's keeping you awake and wishing I could make you warm milk and sit on the edge of your bed until you fell asleep.

I didn't tell you that I feel a little lost sometimes, like a boat whose anchor got up and walked away.

I was scared that you didn't need me anymore.

But that's the part I had to let go of. Because I didn't raise you to stay.

I raised you to rise.

So now, every day, I learn to rise too.

I do it scared. I do it unsure. I do it clumsily sometimes.

But I do it in love.

And if you ever wonder, even for a second, if I'm still here,

I am.

Still cheering. Still proud. Still your mom.

***

I wish I hadn't rushed so much.

It's only now that I realize how many times I said, "Hurry up."

Hurry and eat. Hurry and get dressed. Hurry, the bus is coming. Hurry, you'll be late. Hurry.

I wish I hadn't rushed so much.

Because now? The mornings are slow.

No backpacks by the door. No shoes scattered in the hallway like evidence of a life being lived at full speed. No reason to holler up the stairs about the time.

And I miss it.

I miss the chaos I used to complain about. I miss the noise. I miss the exasperated sighs from the waiting room and even the "Why are you yelling, Mom?" looks that made me feel like the villain in your story.

If I could go back, I'd sit longer while you told that same story for the third time, the one about your friend's drama that seemed earth-shattering to you and trivial to me. I'd laugh slower at your jokes, even the ones that weren't particularly funny. I'd take longer detours on the drive home just to keep you in the car, trapped in conversation with me for a few extra minutes.

But I can't go back.

So I'm learning now to slow down in other ways.

To savor the text that just says "Hey." Or "Checking in." To smile at a meme you send late at night, knowing you thought of me in a random moment. To breathe before I answer your calls, instead of rushing into advice mode before you've even finished explaining the problem.

I'm not in a hurry anymore.

And I hope someday when you slow down too, you'll remember me differently, not as the mom who was always rushing, but the one who eventually learned to stay.

***

I wish I let you see me cry.

I tried to be strong for you.

I thought that's what moms were supposed to do, carry it all, manage it all, smile through it all.

But looking back now, I realize that sometimes my silence may have looked like strength, but it was really just fear hiding behind control.

I didn't want to scare you. I didn't want you to think I didn't have it together.

But maybe, just maybe, you needed to see that even I had breaking points.

Maybe you needed to know that it's okay to cry. That strength isn't pretending, it's showing up anyway.

I wish I let you see the tears I cried when I closed your bedroom door after move-in day, when the reality hit that this room would stay exactly as you left it because there was no one coming home to mess it up.

I wish I told you how my heart cracked a little every time money was tight and there wasn't enough to buy that special thing you wanted. How I'd lie awake calculating and recalculating, wondering if I was teaching you the value of money or just teaching you to expect disappointment.

I wish I told you I missed you so badly it physically hurt, like a constant ache in my chest that I couldn't massage away.

But now I know, it's not too late.

If you ever hear my voice crack, or catch the pause in my breath, just know it's love, not weakness.

I cry because I love you that deep.

***

I wish I told you I still needed you.

There's this myth that once the kids are grown, the parenting stops.

That mothers become obsolete.

That our needs dissolve the moment they spread their wings.

But here's the truth I never said: I still needed you.

Not in the way I did when you were five. Not to pick up your socks or bring me the remote. Not even to tell me every detail of your day.

But I needed to know that I still mattered.

That you remembered.

That somewhere in your day, there was still a space where I belonged.

So, I asked about the test. About the job. About your friends. Not because I'm nosey, but because I still want in.

Even if it's just a sliver.

Because no matter how many years pass, you'll always be a piece of my heart I'll never stop missing.

***

I wish I told you how much you changed me.

Your brothers taught me how to mother, but you taught me how to love someone enough to let them go.

Motherhood broke me wide open, in the best way.

You taught me patience when I didn't think I had any left. You taught me compassion when I didn't feel seen. You taught me how to love without condition, even when I felt empty.

I don't think you'll fully understand how much of me was shaped by raising you.

Not just the tired parts. Not just the proud parts.

But the transformation.

You helped me become more of who I truly am.

The woman who could advocate fiercely for what mattered. The woman who could stay calm in crisis. The woman who could love without expecting anything in return.

And for that ... I will always be grateful.

***

I wish I told you I didn't always know what I was doing.

I know I wore the title like armor.

Mom.

But truthfully?

I was learning as I went.

I Googled. I guessed. I prayed - boy, did I pray. I mimicked what I saw, healed from what I endured, and tried to give you better.

There were moments I got it wrong. Moments I disciplined too harshly or let my stress speak before my heart could.

I wanted you to see me as someone you could depend on, and maybe I confused that with perfection.

But I wish I had told you sooner: I was figuring it out, same as you.

We were both growing, just in different ways.

And if I could do one thing over, I would let you see me learning out loud.

So you'd know it's okay to not have it all together.

It's okay to try, stumble, and try again.

It's okay to be human.

***

I wish I told you about my failures.

I hid the pain of a marriage that ended. The promotions I lost. The mistakes that kept me awake at night.

I wanted you to believe in love, so I hid the complexity of adult relationships.

I wanted you to see me as competent, so I buried the career missteps that taught me my most valuable lessons.

But failure wasn't my enemy. It was my teacher.

Every mistake taught me something I couldn't have learned through success.

If I could go back, I wouldn't hide my failures from you. I'd let you see that stumbling doesn't disqualify you from the race.

Because the woman who never fails never grows.

***

I wish I told you about the unexpected joy.

I was so focused on missing you that I forgot to mention the surprising moments when life felt lighter.

Like the first Monday I woke up to natural light instead of alarms.

The afternoon I bought flowers for myself just because they made me smile.

The travel that healed something I didn't know was broken - standing in foreign markets, tasting freedom in languages I'd never learned.

There was joy in small freedoms too. Eating dinner at whatever time felt right. Watching movies you would have hated.

The deepest joy was discovering I could still surprise myself.

Missing you and finding myself weren't opposites. They were dance partners.

***

I wish I told you I noticed.

I noticed.

Even when I didn't say it.

I noticed the way you tried to be strong when things got hard.

I noticed when you stood up for someone who had no voice.

I noticed the confidence behind your quiet. The questions behind your sarcasm.

I saw the way you softened when no one else was looking.

I noticed how you'd slip extra snacks into your backpack for the kid at school whose lunch was always just a bag of chips. How you'd include the new student who ate alone. How you'd stay after practice to help the younger players even when you were exhausted.

I didn't always say it, but I was watching, and oh, how proud I was.

And still am.

You never needed to be perfect. I just needed to see you try. And you did, more than you'll ever know.

***

I wish I told you that letting go felt like grief.

Everyone talks about the pride.

About watching your child step into the world with confidence, finally free.

They don't talk about the ache.

The slow grief of small goodbyes.

The last school pickup. The final dance recital. The packed bin of childhood memories in the attic.

I wish I told you how many times I cried on the kitchen floor, missing a version of you I'll never see again. The little girl who needed me to cut her food and check for monsters under the bed. The teenager who rolled her eyes at my jokes but still laughed despite herself.

Letting go felt like joy and loss holding hands.

But I did it. Because you were always meant to fly.

And though I grieve the little one I held, I celebrate the person you've become.

Even through the tears.

***

I wish I thanked you for the second chance.

You gave me another beginning.

In loving you, I learned how to love myself.

When I saw your courage, I found mine.

When I watched you face your fears, I whispered to my younger self, "We can still do this."

You gave me purpose in my most uncertain season.

And now?

You've given me permission to dream again.

So thank you.

For showing me that motherhood didn't end, it evolved.

Thank you for letting me walk beside you all those years.

And thank you for being the reason I remembered who I was meant to be.

***

I wish I told you I never stopped praying.

Not once.

Not when you rolled your eyes.

Not when you walked out mid-conversation.

Not even when you said, "I'm fine," with that tone I knew meant you were anything but.

I never stopped.

I prayed when you laughed, and when you didn't call.

I prayed for your safety, your choices, your future family, even the friends I hadn't met yet.

I prayed through your first heartbreak, your college applications, your job interviews. I prayed for the dreams you shared and the ones you kept secret.

My lips may have been silent. But my soul has been in conversation with heaven on your behalf every single day.

You'll never outgrow my prayers.

They'll follow you like breath.

Even when I'm gone.

***

I wish I hadn't measured myself by your mood.

There were days you came home and didn't say much. Days you walked right past me. Days your tone was short or your face unreadable.

And I took it personally.

I measured my worth as a mom by your silence. Your happiness became my report card.

And when you were struggling, I thought I had failed. That I missed something. That I should've done more, known more, fixed more.

But now I see you were growing. And growth is hard.

You were sorting through your own storms, and it wasn't my job to clear every cloud.

I wish I had known that back then. I wish I had given both of us grace.

Because your journey was never meant to be proof of my perfection.

***

I wish I told you that your leaving made space for me too.

At first, all I could see was what I lost.

The missing shoes by the door. The quiet dinner table. The routines that unraveled.

I mourned the version of life where you were the center of my every thought, plan, and prayer.

But what I didn't expect was the space.

The space to think again. To feel again. To dream again.

It came slowly, like sunlight through half-open blinds.

And I began to realize: Your leaving wasn't just the end of something.

It was the beginning of me.

I'll always miss the days when I was your world.

But I'm grateful for the chance to discover who I am when I'm not just your mother.

Turns out, she's someone I actually like.

***

I wish I told you I was sorry about the divorce.

Not sorry that it happened, because some things have to break before they can heal properly.

Sorry that I never asked if you were okay with it.

You were the ones who had to pack bags every other weekend. You became tiny diplomats, making sure neither parent felt left out at school events. You learned to split your stories, your victories, your problems into neat piles that wouldn't make anyone jealous.

I watched you at your college graduation, running between two different sides of the auditorium, making sure you took pictures with both families, trying to spend equal time with everyone so no one felt cheated.

You were twenty years old and still carrying the weight of keeping everyone happy.

I wish I had told you that our happiness wasn't your responsibility.

That you didn't have to protect us from the consequences of decisions we made.

That you were allowed to be angry about having your life split in half, even if the split was necessary.

I'm sorry I put you in charge of keeping the peace.

You deserved to just be our daughter, not our emotional referee.

***

The Words That Matter Now

These are the things I wish I'd said then, Charlie. But maybe saying them now is exactly when they're meant to be heard.

Not just by you, but by every mother who's learning that the hardest conversations are often the ones we have with ourselves.

The truth is, we're all figuring it out as we go. All of us, mothers and daughters, teachers and students, the ones who seem to have it together and the ones who are brave enough to admit they don't.

And maybe that's the most important thing I can tell you now:

It's okay to not have all the words in the moment.

It's okay to say them later.

It's okay to keep learning how to love out loud.

Because love isn't perfected in the saying, it's perfected in the staying.

And I'm still here, Charlie.

Still learning. Still growing. Still your mom.

Just getting better at saying what matters.

***

12

Community Voices

"For where two or three gather in my name, there am I with them." — Matthew 18:20 (KJV)

***

These are the voices of women who've walked this path before you, beside you, and behind you. Each story is shared in her own words, unedited and unfiltered, because sometimes the most powerful truth comes not from perfect prose but from honest hearts.

You are not alone in this journey. These women's experiences span different circumstances, different timelines, different outcomes, but they all share the universal experience of loving someone enough to let them go, and discovering who they are when the letting go is done.

Their voices join yours in the ancient chorus of mothers who've learned that endings are also beginnings, that emptiness can become fullness, and that the heart stretched by love never returns to its original size.

No identity of my own

As parents, do we ever let go? No matter the age, joys or trials, they are secretly why our heart beats!

I have 3 sons. Each 7 years apart; each born at different stages of my life. First one, born during my "Growing" phase; I was young and was still growing into adulthood. I watched my #1 begin to make the transition to manhood when he had children. When he left home, I still had a full house, two remaining at home. I was traveling out of state for work so I feel like I missed a lot of their growing pains; my one regret in life.

I had to push my #2 out of the house (born during my "I'm Grown" phase). His big change over happened when he got married. My #3 (phase "Raising Family") has always been mature for his age, so I didn't know if I was would notice the change. But, Christmas was our day. He would wake me to open gifts. One year he didn't wake me. I was a little crushed. I felt like he grew up overnight.

I had been in the shadows of my husband and/or children; somebody's mom or somebody's wife.

Suddenly, no children and a rocky marriage. I had no name. No identity of my own. Enter phase: "Finding Me"! I found myself fumbling and trying to maintain. Now I have crossed over to phase "Transition". Divorced and mom's caregiver. I have 5 grandchildren and want a name other than grandma. Why am I still in search of me?

— Stephanie

***

Subtle But Necessary Shift In Motherhood

"Do You Ever Really Let Go?

When I was asked to reflect on the moment I let go of my children, I paused and honestly wondered—do we ever really let go? I am 63 years old. My eldest daughter is 30, and my youngest is 28, and even now, I find myself emotionally intertwined with their lives. There are moments when I realize I'm still holding on—still connected, still invested, sometimes even living my life through theirs.

What I've learned, though, is that there is a subtle but necessary shift in motherhood. At some point, I had to move from mothering to mentoring—from telling them what to do, to advising when asked. And that wasn't easy. One day, I realized I had become so wrapped up in their lives that I had neglected parts of my own. I was trapped in a role that had defined me for so long. And in order to set them free, I had to first set myself free.

So, I began to let go—not of love, but of control. And in that process, I found pieces of myself that had long been buried under the weight of constant nurturing. I discovered that yes, I am a mother—but I am also so much more. I uncovered a passion for cooking and realized I was a talented chef. I stepped into the world of entrepreneurship and built a business that reflected my creativity and spirit. I became a motivator and encourager, not just to my children, but to others around me.

And perhaps the most surprising discovery of all—I found me. I shed over 53 pounds of "mothering weight," both physically and emotionally. I reconnected with the woman I was before children, and the woman I had become because of them. She was beautiful, bold, and ready to live.

I remember talking to friends who had already faced the empty nest season—some couples survived, others did not. That scared me. So my husband and I decided to be proactive. We started date nights before our daughters even left home. We practiced what life would look like with just the two of us, and to our surprise, we got good at it. We leaned into each other. We talked. We laughed. We rebuilt our friendship.

Last July 2nd, we celebrated 30 years of marriage—now approaching 31—and I can honestly say we are enjoying our best life yet in this new season of empty nest and retirement.

Letting go isn't a single moment—it's a series of heart-surrenders. And what's stayed with me most is this: you don't lose your children when they grow up—you gain a new version of them, and a new version of yourself, too."

— Abbie Huckleby

***

Positioning Ourselves To Reclaim Our Lives

"One day, I came to realize that letting go of a child, after investing considerable time and energy, is a challenging yet crucial aspect of the parent-child relationship. It requires trusting their independence, enabling them to make their own decisions, and accepting that they will eventually navigate life on their own terms.

From the moment both our children were born, my husband and I dedicated ourselves to nurturing and supporting them. We often made sacrifices to ensure they had a strong foundation for becoming independent self-sufficient, and Christ-centered. We wanted them to carry the morals, values, and lessons that we instilled in them as children into adulthood.

We actively invested time, energy, and resources into their growth and development. We encouraged their interests, fostered emotional intelligence, instilled a growth mindset, and nurtured their dreams. We also modeled positive behaviors and attitudes. Essentially, we poured into our children, being present, actively involved, and creating a supportive environment where they could thrive. We sacrificed ourselves, investing in their future and helping them to develop into the well-rounded, confident and compassionate individuals that they are today.

Now that our children are grown and responsible adults, we have become selfish with our time and resources. We're looking ahead to our retirement years and have shifted our priorities away from raising children to focusing on our own needs, interests, and well-being.

The love that we have for our children remains as strong as it was the day that each was born, and it will never die. After pouring into them for so many years, letting them go hasn't been easy. But, we are now more focused on what lies ahead in our future and positioning ourselves to reclaim our lives, both as individuals and as a couple."

— *Val Baker*

***

Emotionally Taxing ... A Very Sad Time.

"That little voice in my head constantly saying to me 'I am good enough for you.'

Dropping off my children to their respective colleges was emotionally taxing for me. Knowing it's the final letting go into the world. Also knowing that I am now stuck with a partner at home who is emotionally unstable, uncaring, and was just using me for his benefits, especially financial support. It was a very sad time. But at the same time it was a powerful time to reassess my relationship with God who kept telling me in that quiet voice that He would take care of my children but I Now need to give it all to Him because HE IS GOOD ENOUGH FOR ME. As soon as I slowly started yielding everything to God, without caring what others would say, I started to finally feel better about making my own decisions without guilt and creating my own happiness.

I wish I had known earlier on that I did not have to manage relationships that were not good for me. "Whatever you manage will damage you." I was in this damaged state for a long time. The unfortunate thing was that I knew all along but was too ashamed to admit it or do anything about it.

Listening to God's directions and taking one day at a time has been the most rewarding experience of my life so far. I am still a work in progress but I am much happier now and relying on God every minute of the day."

— *Anonymous*

Nothing prepares you for the emptiness that sneaks in

I can still feel the door click shut behind me, Lauren stood there in her new dorm room, a little nervous, a lot excited, surrounded by boxes and bedding and plans for the future. I hugged her tightly, longer than she probably wanted, and whispered how proud I was. I smiled as I backed away. I smiled even as my heart cracked wide open.

You spend years preparing your child for this, cheering them on, teaching them to be strong, independent, kind. But nothing prepares you for the moment you leave them behind. Nothing prepares you for the emptiness that sneaks in when you get back into your car alone.

What surprised me most was the mix of pride and heartbreak. I had done my job, she was ready, but I wasn't ready for how much I would miss the small, everyday pieces of our life together.

And then, midway through Lauren's freshman year, the letting go deepened. Her father and I ended our marriage after 22 years. It was agonizing. I never wanted to break up our family. But after all the years of telling Lauren to follow her heart and stay true to herself, I realized I wasn't living by the same words. Letting go of my marriage, the life we had built, was another kind of grief, layered on top of the first.

What has stayed with me is this: letting go isn't one sudden moment. It's a thousand quiet choices to love deeply, even as things change. You don't lose your child when you leave them at school; you build a new kind of relationship across the distance. And sometimes, in the process, you find your own way home to yourself.

If I could tell someone else standing at that dorm room door: it's okay to feel both broken and proud. Love makes space for both.

— Stephanie Whalen

***

A time you let go (and what it cost or gifted you)

I have watched my son go off into the world more than once.

As a divorced mother who lived in a different state from my ex-husband, I remember having alternate holidays with my son. Then one day my son said, "I know how you do things, I want to see how a man does things." He then went to live with his father. I was so devastated I couldn't think straight. When it came time to take him to the airport, I honestly got lost and he had to catch a later flight. A year later I found a job closer and he came to live with me in the same city with his Dad.

The second time is when he graduated from high school and went to the military. That time I was proud and hopeful. However, his leaving always would bring me to my knees to pray for him. The next time was when he went to college many hours away from me. I was proud and hopeful for him as I am now.

So, I fill my days with work. And I desperately try to run my life now instead of always trying to run his life. He is an adult now. And his absence leaves me to face myself and turn to my next chapter. Attempting to shower love on myself the way I have always tried to do for my son.

— Ouida McAfee

***

The Chorus Continues

These voices represent just a fraction of the women who've walked this path. Each story is unique, yet the threads that connect them are universal: the love that shapes us, the letting go that transforms us, and the discovery that we are more than the roles we've played.

In boardrooms and coffee shops, in church pews and grocery store aisles, in quiet moments of reflection and conversations with friends, women everywhere are navigating this power shift. Some with grace, some with struggle, most with a mixture of both.

What matters is not how perfectly we handle the letting go, but how courageously we embrace what comes next. These women's stories remind us that there is no single right way to move through this season, no perfect timeline for healing, no standard script for discovery.

There is only the journey itself, made sacred by the love that began it and the hope that sustains it.

Your voice belongs in this chorus. Your story matters. Your struggle is valid. Your growth is witnessed.

And wherever you are in this journey—whether you're just beginning to see the horizon of change or you're years into your new normal—know that you are not alone.

The community of women who understand this passage is vast and welcoming. We've saved a place for you in our circle, reserved a chair at our table, kept a light on for your arrival.

Because some journeys are meant to be traveled in the company of others who've walked the path before you.

Across the world, mothers are performing this same ritual of letting go. We're all learning to love with open hands instead of closed fists. We're discovering that what feels like individual heartbreak is actually collective transformation waiting to be recognized.

Welcome to the sisterhood of mothers who've learned that loving deeply means letting go completely, and that letting go completely opens us to becoming more than we ever imagined possible.

Your Third Act is waiting.

13

Where It All Began

The Letter That Started Everything

There's something you should know about everything you just read. It started with tears in a coffee shop.

Not elegant tears, the kind that come with warning and can be gracefully dabbed away. These were the raw, uncontrollable kind that ambush you in public places and refuse to be reasoned with. The kind that make strangers approach with tissues and gentle words because grief this visible demands witness.

I was sitting in a popular coffee shop in Crofton, Maryland, my notebook open, pen in hand, watching other people's ordinary afternoons unfold around me. Mothers with strollers navigating between tables, their toddlers' voices mixing with the hiss of espresso machines. Students with textbooks spread like fortresses around their laptops, highlighters bleeding yellow across pages I'd never see. Business people with urgent phone calls, their voices clipped with the efficiency of people who had places to be and problems to solve.

Everyone moving through their lives with purpose while I sat preparing for what felt like the end of mine.

This was supposed to be simple. The school tradition, write a letter to your child for their senior retreat, something meaningful to be delivered during this pivotal moment before they step into adulthood. A tradition meant to leave a lasting impression, a milestone wrapped in paper and ink.

But what poured out wasn't just a letter. It was a soul offering.

I'd come to that coffee shop thinking I'd write something encouraging but contained. Something maternal but measured. Something that would make her feel loved without making me feel exposed.

But the moment I put pen to paper, something broke open. Not just the tears, though they came harder with each word, but something deeper. The recognition that what I was feeling was too big for silence, too important for keeping to myself, too universal for shame.

Seventeen years of motherhood came flooding out in a torrent I couldn't control. Every 3 AM worry that had kept me staring at the ceiling. Every prayer whispered over her sleeping form. Every moment of fierce pride mixed with terrifying love. Every lesson I'd tried to teach but wasn't sure had landed. Every piece of wisdom I'd gathered like a squirrel storing nuts for the winter that was coming, the winter of her independence.

I wrote through tears that blurred my handwriting. I wrote until my hand cramped and my coffee grew cold. I wrote until the coffee shop began to empty around me and baristas started cleaning tables with the patient efficiency of people waiting for the last customer to leave.

I wrote until every ache had words, until every blessing had been spoken, until every fear had been faced and surrendered to the only One who could hold them.

And in that coffee shop, surrounded by the debris of other people's ordinary days, I found myself doing what I'd done through every season of motherhood: giving thanks. Even in the breaking. Especially in the breaking.

The gratitude prayer poured out like water from a broken dam, washing over every fear with the certainty that I wasn't walking into this unknown alone. I was walking with the God who had carried us both this far and wouldn't stop now.

I opened my notebook and began to write. Not to the world. Not for a book. Just to her. Just from the overflowing of a mother's heart that had run out of tomorrows to say these things in person.

The letter poured out like prayer, like testimony, like bleeding. Every fear I couldn't voice. Every hope I couldn't guarantee. Every truth I'd learned through seventeen years of loving someone more than breathing. Every piece of wisdom I'd gathered for this exact moment, the moment when love means letting go.

When I finished, I knew I'd written the most important thing I'd ever written. Not because it was eloquent, it wasn't. But because it was true. Raw. Unfiltered. The kind of honesty that can only come when you're willing to break open in public and trust that love is stronger than embarrassment.

I dropped that letter off at school the next day, watching it disappear into the administrative process that would deliver it to Charlie during her retreat. I had no idea it would become the foundation for everything that followed, this book, this journey, this understanding that sometimes the most private pain becomes the most public purpose.

For years, that letter lived in private. Charlie carried it to California, and I carried the memory of writing it through every season that followed. Through my own transformation in Houston. Through learning to pray from a distance. Through discovering my Third Act. Through all the growth that you've witnessed in these pages.

But as I met other mothers, in grocery stores and gas stations, at airports and coffee shops, I kept hearing the same story. The same ache. The same beautiful, terrible, universal experience of watching the person you love most walk toward a life that doesn't center around you.

And I began to understand that the letter wasn't just mine. It belonged to every mother who has ever stood at the threshold between holding on and letting go.

When Love Gets Complicated

But let me be clear; not every mother-child relationship unfolds like a beautiful story tied with a bow. Ours certainly didn't. There were tensions, misunderstandings, cultural collisions between my African heritage and her American experience. There were moments of friction, periods of distance, times when love felt complicated and messy and hard.

Some relationships are fraught with ongoing conflict. Some mothers and daughters find themselves separated by wounds too deep for easy healing, living in silence where words once flowed freely. Some find themselves loving from a much greater distance, not by choice, but by necessity, their hearts carrying love that has no safe place to land.

If you're one of those mothers reading this whose children won't receive letters, whose relationships exist in the space of prayer rather than presence, who love from distances measured not in miles but in silence, this story is for you too. The power of loving when you cannot reach, of blessing when you cannot speak, of mothering when you cannot touch, this is holy work that matters just as much.

Love finds a way, even when words cannot.

And yet, even in the most broken relationships, one thing remains unbroken: a mother's love. Your letter might be a prayer instead of prose. Your blessing might be whispered in private instead of written on paper. But the love is still there, still powerful, still transformative.

The wisdom you've read in these chapters? It grew from seeds planted in that coffee shop letter. The frameworks and insights, the spiritual truths and practical realities, they all trace back to that moment when a breaking heart became a flowing pen.

This book exists because one mother's private pain became public permission for others to feel, to heal, to become.

The letter you're about to read is exactly as I wrote it that day, tears, hope, terror, faith, typos, imperfect grammar, and all. I haven't polished it or updated it or made it prettier. Because the power was never in perfection. It was in authenticity.

You'll recognize themes you've encountered throughout this book. But here, they're raw. Unprocessed. Written not from the safety of hindsight but from the dangerous edge of present-tense love.

You'll see the DNA of everything we've explored together, the faith before freedom, the prayer from a distance, the blessing forward, the Third Act calling. But you'll see it as it was born: in desperation, in surrender, in the sacred space where love meets letting go.

This is where the journey you've just taken began. In the broken-open heart of one mother who didn't know if she'd survive watching her daughter fly.

She did survive. She thrived. She transformed.

But first, she had to write her way through the fear.

***

My Dearest JoAnna,

Wow! Where did the time go? Yesterday you were a kid, today you have turned into a gorgeous brilliant young lady. And confident too. Am I proud to call you my daughter or what? Watch out world here comes my Charlie :)

I'm glad for this opportunity to put some of my feelings for you in writing. I'm sure you already know you are loved unconditionally that means even when you're acting your age :(. I also wanted to let you what an absolute joy you have been and how much you mean to me. Can you imagine my life without you? Ok, I'll try not to think about next year (I already have a solution...visit often). I know without the shadow of a doubt that you're going places. I believe with all my heart that you will someday become famous. So here are some more "life lessons" as we've dubbed it:

1. *God first. Always. Always. Always. No matter who you meet along the way of life and you will meet many different types of people. From friends, acquaintances, coworkers, event relationships. Each and all relationships teaches us something What you're exposed to. Put God first. Seeking God by yourself not thru others there is a personal intimate relationship. He formed you and knows the strands of hair on your head. There is only 1 God. Seek Him.*

2. *Your mind is a phenomenal tool. Use it. The first battleground and victory ground is the human mind. Win any and all battles in your mind and you are, you will be victorious. Use your mind to dream BIG, HUMONGOUS dreams. If your dream for your future doesn't scare you it's too small. Dream the kind of dreams that will take God's intervention to manifest. Remember that song... Believe in the unbelievable, receive the inconceivable and see beyond your wildest imagination? Remember? Well that was my*

mantra let your imagination soar. If you can see it in your mind. You can do it.

3. *Love Jo first and foremost, above everyone else. Don't allow anyone to define you. If you love yourself, no one can put you down or tell you what you can and cannot do. You are unstoppable.*

4. *Curveballs and Lemons. As long as there are gray patches in the sky there'd be curveballs and lemons. So when life throws you a curveball, go after it with a single unshakeable focus... home run! It doesn't matter how many tries it takes, just go after it. You will win. Guaranteed! And if that challenge is a lemon, my dear girl, add sugar and make lemonade. My point is there will be challenges along the way, but it will NOT overtake you*

   Isaiah 43: 2-3

   Jeremiah 5:22

   It simply cannot overtake you as long as you don't quit in your mind first. Cry in the shower if you must, but know in your head and in your mind you are the winner.

5. *Travel around the world. Not just as a tourist but purposefully to behold the wonders and beauty of God. Enjoy his creation, his beauty in everything and everyone. Everything you see was first conceived in somebody's mind and they saw it through, that my dear is the joy in traveling. To truly see. Open your eyes, see, smell, touch and know you are unstoppable. And wherever the sole of your feet shall touch, you will possess it.*

6. *Financial pillar. Don't let go of your dream to be a giver, to make a difference in other people's lives. Remember it started in your mind don't let it go until it becomes a reality. Start with what's in your hand today. Give of the little you have and watch God multiply your seed. Don't wait, it starts now. It doesn't have to be money, it can be service. But give.*

7. *Concerning college, I know that we've made plans but don't forget that all things work together for the good, to them that love God, to them that are called according to <u>his purposes</u> so we have aimed for the stars. Now we give thanks for the perfect place where he has prepared for you. Give thanks in your mind, with your mouth <u>before</u> the admissions letters begin to arrive. Show your gratitude.*

And finally my darling JoAnna, fall in love! Hopelessly, madly in love. It is the most beautiful thing. Even if you make a mistake, fall in love again, like you never lost before. And dance, each and everything you get a chance, <u>dance</u>! It doesn't matter who with or alone just dance. It's an automatic cure for tons of ailments.

Now go have fun and be a kid. Enjoy it because adulthood is overrated. It's only filled with responsibilities and bills. Don't be in a hurry. Enjoy your teenage years.

I love you with all my heart JoAnna Izon and I wouldn't trade you for all the monies in the entire world.

Go get them Charlie! Go get them Madam President!!

Mom

***

Sacred Transformation

Ten years have passed since I wrote those words in a coffee shop, my heart breaking and reforming with every sentence.

JoAnna kept that letter through her years at USC, through early career challenges, through relationships and relocations and all the changes I could only witness from a distance. But here's what I've learned since then: the letter didn't just guide her. Writing it transformed me.

After writing this letter to my daughter, I realized that words once written have a life beyond our intentions. What began as a mother's outpouring of love became a testimony to God's faithfulness through every season of motherhood. Those raw words on the page became the foundation for everything you've read in this book. The themes I explored in private became the wisdom I could share in public. The faith I whispered to one daughter became hope I could offer to millions of mothers.

The pain I was afraid would destroy me became the source of purpose I never could have imagined.

My Anchor in Every Storm

One of my deepest prayers of thanksgiving is simply gratitude for the challenges that have kept me on my knees, hands raised in surrender to a God who has proven Himself faithful. My life's anchor scripture, Jeremiah 5:22, never promised absence of storms, it actually foretold them. The waves would come, the seas would roar, but God established a "perpetual decree," unchangeable and immovable until the end of eternity. The waters may rise, but they cannot, will not overtake those who trust in Him.

When all evidence points to the contrary, I return to this promise and respectfully remind God of His word. Has my journey been easy? No. Like yours, my path has wound through peaks and valleys. But in those valleys, especially the deep shadows of letting go, I discovered an anchor that held firm when everything else shifted.

This letter captured a sacred moment of transition, both for my daughter and for me. In writing it, I was not just preparing her for the world; I was preparing myself to release her into it. Every word became both a benediction and a bridge, blessing her forward while creating a connection that distance couldn't diminish.

Years later, when I asked JoAnna's permission to share our letter with the world, to turn it into this book, she gave me the same gift she'd given me in Houston: permission to live my own life fully. "Mom," she said, "if it helps other mothers and daughters understand each other better, then it should be shared."

Once again, my daughter was teaching me about freedom - this time, the freedom to transform private pain into public purpose.

The Letter That's Haunting You Right Now

Here's what I know about you, dear reader: As you read my imperfect, typo-filled, grammatically flawed letter to JoAnna, something stirred in your chest. A recognition. An ache. A whisper that said, "I need to write my own."

That whisper isn't accidental. It's sacred. It's your heart recognizing that somewhere in your own story, there are words that need to be written. Love that needs to be expressed. Truth that needs to be spoken before time runs out. And time is running out. Not because the world is ending, but because children grow up. Because relationships shift. Because the moment when your words could matter most is closer than you think.

Right now, as you sit reading this, your letter is already forming in your heart. The words you've been too afraid to say. The love you've been too embarrassed to express. The wisdom you've gathered through your own journey of loving someone more than breathing.

Maybe it's a letter to your child who's leaving soon, your chance to put on paper everything you hope they'll remember when they forget to call home.

Maybe it's a letter to the one who left years ago but has never heard these particular truths from you, words that could heal old wounds or build new bridges.

Maybe it's a letter to the one who isn't your biological child but carries your heart nonetheless, chosen love deserves chosen words.

Maybe it's a letter to yourself, the woman who gave so much of herself to raising others that she forgot she was worth writing to.

Here's what I want you to understand: if you feel called to write a letter but you don't, it will haunt you. That stirring in your chest will become a permanent ache. The words that want to be born will keep knocking at your heart's door, asking why you didn't give them life when you had the chance.

Years from now, when your child is facing storms you can't weather for them, you'll remember this moment. You'll remember that you could have written words that would anchor them, but you chose silence instead.

Years from now, when relationships have shifted and opportunities have passed, you'll remember that you could have spoken love into existence, but fear held your pen hostage. The regret of words left unspoken is a heavier burden than the vulnerability of words shared poorly.

Call To Action

This isn't just an invitation to write your own letter. This is love calling you to action. This is your heart insisting that some things are too important for "someday."

Consider these elements as you write, but don't let structure constrain spirit:

Affirm who they are, not just what they've accomplished. Remind them of the qualities you've seen grow in them that will serve them well beyond any classroom or career.

Share wisdom you wish you'd known at their age, not as regret but as gift, the perspective that only life experience can bring.

Express your faith in their journey, acknowledging that while their path may differ from what you imagined, you trust the unique purpose that exists for their life.

193

Release them from expectations that might burden rather than bless. Let them know your love isn't conditional on following a prescribed path.

Offer an anchor truth that can guide them through uncertain waters, whether it's a scripture, a family saying, a life principle, or wisdom that has anchored your own journey through storms.

Include your thanksgiving prayer, the gratitude that transforms every fear into faith, every worry into worship.

Your letter need not be perfect or poetic. It simply needs to be authentic, written from that place where your heart meets truth. The words that flow from this sacred space will carry power beyond what you can imagine.

Write it by hand if possible. Something happens in the connection between heart, mind, and pen that technology cannot replicate. The imperfections, crossed-out words, smudged ink from tears, become part of its beauty and authenticity.

This tradition costs nothing but time and courage, yet it creates a legacy more valuable than any material gift. Your words become a lighthouse they can return to throughout their journey, a reminder of where they came from and who has always believed in their potential.

And when you're finished, when you've poured your heart onto paper and blessed them forward with words that will outlast your presence, you'll discover what I did. The letter you thought you were writing for them becomes the letter you needed to write for yourself.

The healing you thought you were offering becomes the healing you receive. The blessing you thought you were giving becomes the blessing that sets you free to become whoever you're meant to be next. This is where transformation begins. With one brave mother willing to put love into words that echo long after voices fade.

Your Time Is Now

In a world of digital communication that disappears with a swipe, a letter remains tangible, preservable, a testament to love that endures beyond the daily letting go.

Your letter is waiting.

Your words are forming.

Your love is calling for expression.

Don't let fear rob your children of the lighthouse they need for their journey. Don't let "someday" steal the power of "today."

The coffee shop moment that changed my life forever started with one sentence: "My Dearest JoAnna..."

What will your first sentence be?

The pen is in your hand. The paper is waiting. The love is overflowing.

Write it.

Your heart won't let you rest until you do.

Epilogue: The Story Continues

Ten years ago, I stood barefoot on cold asphalt, chasing a garbage truck in my pajamas, certain I was losing my mind.

Today, I'm writing these words from my home office in Maryland, where I've built a life that honors both my roots and my wings. My mother lives with my sister, just a walking distance from me, while my father is about thirty minutes away. My daughter calls from California with news about her latest adventure. My sons have grown into remarkable men, each building their own path with the strength and wisdom I prayed they'd carry into the world.

The Third Act didn't end when I thought I had figured out who I was after my children left. It evolved, deepened, expanded into something I never could have imagined. I'm still learning to parent adult children without trying to parent them, a delicate dance of love and letting go that requires constant recalibration. I've discovered friendships that exist for their own sake, not because our children played together. I've traveled to places I'd dreamed of visiting when I was too busy driving to football practice to imagine solo adventures, and I continue to explore this wide world with the wonder of someone who's finally free to follow her curiosity.

But more than anything, I've learned that the Third Act isn't about closure, it's about opening. Opening to possibilities I never considered, relationships I never expected, aspects of myself I never knew existed.

What I've discovered is that transformation accelerates when it's shared. The women in those Houston coffee shops weren't just processing their own identity shifts, they were witnessing each other's courage and realizing their struggles weren't unique failures but universal passages. Every story shared became permission for someone else to speak their truth. Every breakthrough celebrated became proof that change was possible for all of us.

The letters I encouraged women to write to their children became letters they needed to write to themselves. The frameworks I developed from my own fumbling became tools other women could adapt to their circumstances. The community that started as my personal lifeline evolved into something larger, a network of women who understand that our most transformative years aren't behind us, they're unfolding right now.

This is how lasting change happens, not in isolation but in the company of others walking similar paths. When one woman admits she doesn't know who she is without children to manage, it gives another woman permission to say the same. When one woman takes a photography class after twenty years, it reminds another woman that her abandoned dreams are still valid. When one woman travels solo for the first time, it expands what other women believe possible for themselves.

The power isn't just in your individual transformation. It's in becoming part of a movement of women who refuse to disappear when their traditional roles shift. Women who understand that sharing our lived experiences isn't just therapeutic, it's revolutionary. We're proving that the wisdom earned through decades of loving others can be channeled into loving ourselves and each other with the same fierce devotion.

Your story matters because it gives someone else permission to write theirs. Your transformation matters because it expands what other women believe possible. Your courage to begin again matters because it lights the path for women still standing at their own thresholds, wondering if they're brave enough to step through.

This is how we change the narrative about women and aging, about mothers and relevance, about dreams deferred and possibilities discovered. One story at a time. One transformation at a time. One community at a time.

This book isn't the end of my story. It's a progress report from the middle of an ongoing transformation.

Writing this ten years later, I can tell you the Third Act doesn't end with one decision or one move or one revelation. I'm completing the final chapters of this manuscript from a hotel room in Dublin, Ireland, part of my ongoing travel transformation that would have been impossible during the carpool years. The YouTube channel I started to share these insights has reached over 30,000 views, creating conversations with women across six continents.

Ten years in, I'm still transforming. Still questioning. Still choosing growth over certainty. The woman who stood barefoot chasing garbage trucks has learned to chase possibilities instead.

Now in my early sixties, a full decade into this Third Act journey, I'm still growing, still discovering, still saying yes to invitations I might have declined in my twenties for fear of not being ready.

The Third Act has taught me that waiting for readiness is the enemy of remarkable. Courage is what creates transformation. And courage, like every muscle worth building, grows stronger with each act of faith.

So to every woman reading this: your Third Act isn't waiting for you to be ready, it's demanding you begin. Not when you have all the answers, but when you're brave enough to live the questions. Not when you're perfect, but when you're present to the magnificent, messy, ongoing work of becoming the woman you were always meant to be.

The story continues. Your story continues. And I can't wait to see what you become.

Join the Movement

If this book has stirred something in you, a recognition, a hope, a holy restlessness, you're not meant to walk this path alone.

The Third Act Society is a growing community of women who refuse to believe that their best chapters are behind them. We're building something beautiful together, a space where women can share wisdom, encouragement, and the kind of authentic connection that comes from understanding this sacred transition.

What we're creating together:

- Online connection through multiple platforms
- Resources for every stage of the Third Act journey
- A safe space to share your struggles and celebrate your victories
- Access to workshops, discussions, and exclusive content
- Growing network of women who understand this journey

Share your story: Use #ThirdActMotherhood to connect with women worldwide who are writing their own Third Acts.

Ready for Your Next Chapter?

The Trillion-Dollar Recognition

If you recognized yourself in these pages, you're already part of the most underestimated economic force on the planet.

While you were reading this book, 73 million women worldwide stood at the threshold of their highest earning potential, their peak investment years, their maximum wealth-building decades. Women controlling $15 trillion in global wealth, finally entering the life phase where they get to spend their money on their own dreams instead of everyone else's needs..

The corporate world calls us "empty nesters" and expects us to step aside. The economy treats us like we're disappearing just when we're gaining the confidence, connections, and capital to change everything.

But here's what they missed: We're not disappearing. We're consolidating power.

Every culture teaches women our age to shrink. To volunteer quietly. To support others' dreams while whispering our own. But what if everything we learned about this season was designed to keep us small precisely because they know how dangerous we become when we realize our worth?

The letter I wrote for my daughter's senior class retreat tradition was supposed to be simple. But when I sat down to write, my heart poured out onto the paper. I was weeping by the time I finished - not from sadness, but from finally hearing my own voice after years of silence. That letter became this book. This book is becoming a movement. And this movement is becoming the economic shift that changes how the world sees women like us.

Because when 73 million women decide to stop spending their money on everyone else's priorities and start investing in their own power? When we stop working for other people's companies and start building our own enterprises? When we stop supporting other people's movements and start leading our own?

The economy shifts. Permanently.

The Economic Transformation

You want to know what transformation really looks like? It creates value.

The Third Act Society isn't just a community, it's what happens when women stop waiting for permission to use their voices. Every woman who writes her letter discovers she has something to say. Every story shared becomes permission for another woman to tell hers. Every book passed along becomes an invitation for someone else to step into her power, start her own circle, take up the space she's always deserved.

This is how economic empowerment actually works: We build wealth by building each other up.

Right now, women are starting to understand what happens when we stop spending our energy on everyone else's dreams and start investing in our own. They're discovering that the wisdom earned through raising children, managing households, and navigating life transitions has commercial value in a world that desperately needs what we know. They're finding that organizations, and the men who lead many of them, especially those who raised daughters and understand our strength, are finally ready to pay for the kind of leadership development that only comes from lived experience.

They're turning personal breakthrough into purposeful impact.

The framework you just learned, the path from letter to transformation to leadership, creates opportunities for women who thought their most valuable years were behind them. When you understand how to navigate major life transitions, you possess something organizations desperately need. When you know how to help other women find their voices, you hold expertise that has never been more valued.

The movement is profitable because the need is massive, the market is underserved, and we have the solution.

Here's what becomes possible: Lead a Third Act Society circle in your community. Share this framework with women who need what you've learned. Apply to facilitate workshops for organizations finally ready to support women through life transitions that every workplace faces but few know how to handle.

The infrastructure is growing. The need is massive. The invitation is open.

Write your letter, that's your personal transformation.

Buy copies of this book in bulk, that's your first commercial action.

Start your local Third Act Society circle, that's your leadership in action. Help other women discover their own paths, that's your expertise in practice. Build the movement that changes how women are valued, that's our transformation.

This isn't just about changing your life. It's about changing the economy. And it starts with your letter.

Ready to lead? Join the founding community at thirdactsociety.com/circles

Write your story. Build your business. Change the world.

The Third Act Ecosystem

Tools to support your transformation journey

THRIVE METHODS + PROGRAMS

If this book stirred something in you, a recognition, a hope, a quiet knowing that your story isn't finished, you're not meant to figure out what comes next alone.

After living my own Third Act transformation for over a decade, I've learned that inspiration without tools often leads to frustration. You feel the call to change, but you don't know where to start. You have dreams, but no clear path forward.

The THRIVE Method grew from my own journey of moving from lost to found, from reactive to intentional, from surviving my identity shift to thriving in it.

The Framework That Changed Everything:

T - **Truth Assessment:** Getting honest about where you are.

H - **Horizon Mapping:** Envisioning what's possible with intention.

R - **Resource Recognition:** Recognizing what you already have

I - **Implementation Strategy:** Creating plans that work with real life

V - **Validation and Adjustment:** Regular check-ins and course corrections

E - Evolution Mindset: Embracing the ongoing process of becoming

Where to Begin:

THRIVE Method Quick Start *(Free)*

Start with the first two components of the framework, the same tools that helped me move from that coffee shop breakdown to purposeful living.

Includes:

- Truth Assessment exercises
- Horizon Mapping worksheets
- Gentle guidance for your first steps forward

21 Days to Your Next Chapter *($97)*

If you're ready for more structure and community support, this step-by-step program guides you through the complete THRIVE Method over three weeks.

THRIVE Method for Personal Life *($297)*

The comprehensive framework for women ready to approach their Third Act with the same strategic thinking they bring to other important areas of their lives.

Book readers receive special pricing with code: **THIRDACT**

Because reading about transformation is beautiful. But living it? That's everything.

Your next chapter is calling. When you're ready, I'm here to help you write it.

Coming Soon:

- Third Act Living journals with guided prompts
- "Letters to My Future Self" stationery collections
- Coffee mugs featuring book quotes for daily inspiration
- Study guides designed for church and book club discussions
- Workshop and retreat materials

Acknowledgements

The village that raised this book spans continents and generations.

To my parents, you opened pathways from Lagos to America's endless possibilities. Your choices, however complex, gave us the foundation to dream beyond borders and believe that oceans couldn't limit what we could achieve.

To Sister mi, one of my biggest cheerleaders, you opened the door that led to everything beautiful that followed. From childhood dreams to midlife transformations, you've held my hand through every crossing, making me brave enough to keep walking forward.

To my siblings, the tight-knit circle that proved family means showing up for each other no matter what. The bond we share transcends distance and time, rooted in the understanding that we're not just related, we're chosen family who would choose each other again and again.

To the schools that opened doors when my faith was bigger than my bank account, Grace Christian School in Bowie, Maryland, and Archbishop Spalding High School in Severn, Maryland. Your grace changed the trajectory of our lives and reminded me that sometimes the most important investments are the ones made in mothers who are still working toward their dreams despite the challenges.

To my pastors and spiritual mothers who carried me in prayer when my own faith felt too fragile to hold, your hands lifted me to God's throne when I couldn't find the words, the strength, or even the will to pray for myself. You saw me through seasons when I was too broken to know I was breaking, too lost to realize I needed finding. Your intercession became my lifeline, your faith became my bridge back to hope. I will never forget how you loved me through the wilderness years with the patience of those who truly understand God's heart for His daughters.

To the mentors who saw potential in me when I couldn't see past my pain, and to the friends who stayed close when I wasn't easy to love, your faithfulness taught me what it means to be held by community even when you feel unworthy of the holding.

To my Houston sisters - Carol, Raquel, Renee and Abby - who proved that family isn't just who you're born to but who you choose to become alongside. You showed me that community can be created anywhere by women brave enough to be honest about their struggles.

To the mothers who shared their stories with me, in coffee shops and grocery store aisles, in text messages sent at 2 AM, in tearful phone calls that lasted hours. Your honesty gave me permission to tell this story. Your trust gave me courage to tell it truthfully.

To the women in my Third Act Society community, you transformed my personal healing into collective hope. You proved that this journey is better traveled together.

To my three children, you each taught me different dimensions of love and showed me what it means to pour your whole heart into raising human beings who will surpass everything you ever imagined for them. While this book explores my midlife transformation through the lens of Charlie's departure as my last child, please know that every lesson I learned as your mother, every moment of joy and challenge we shared, every way you each stretched my heart and shaped my character lives in these pages. You made me a mother, and then, in the beautiful, terrifying act of growing into your own lives, you helped me remember I was always meant to be a woman too. Every word in this book is wrapped in love that never stopped growing, even when the way I showed it had to evolve.

And to every mother who has ever stood at the threshold of goodbye, knowing that loving well means letting go, this book exists because you exist. Your tears at college drop-offs, your middle-of-the-night worries, your questions about who you are when you're no longer needed every day, all of it matters. All of it is holy. All of it led to this moment when one mother decided to stop suffering in silence and start building the community where none of us has to walk this sacred, difficult path alone. Your courage inspired mine. Your stories became our story. Your willingness to keep loving, keep growing, keep believing that your best years aren't behind you, that's what makes this movement possible.

About the author

Aderonke 'Ronnie' Izon is the founder of Third Act Society, a community dedicated to helping women transform their midlife transition into their most vibrant chapter yet. After her own challenging empty nest experience, Ronnie developed the THRIVE Method and Permission Framework to help women break free from limiting beliefs and create meaningful Third Acts.

Born in Lagos, Nigeria, and boarding school educated in Nigeria through high school before pursuing higher education in America, Ronnie brings a unique cultural perspective to the universal experience of motherhood and midlife transition. After two decades and 206,000 miles of carpools, practices, and performances, she found herself in the unexpected position of having to rediscover who she was when she wasn't actively mothering.

Her journey from feeling erased to Third Act empowerment has taken her from Maryland to Houston and back to Maryland, proving that the Third Act isn't about settling down - it's about rising up. A mother of three who navigated her own transformation when her youngest daughter left for college at 17, Ronnie understands firsthand the complex emotions of letting go while holding on to love.

Before discovering her Third Act Society calling, Ronnie spent over twenty years in information security and risk management, helping companies navigate major transitions - skills that proved invaluable when navigating her own life transformation.

Her popular YouTube series including "Permission" and "Find Your Joy Again" have touched thousands of women struggling with identity, purpose, and fulfillment after 50. Through her courses, coaching, and community, Ronnie guides women to reclaim their power, rediscover their passions, and reimagine what's possible in this vital stage of life.

Her writing combines raw honesty with spiritual wisdom, offering both comfort and challenge to women ready to write their next chapter. When she's not writing or speaking, Ronnie can be found planning her next solo adventure (South Korea, Vietnam and Japan are on the horizon), taking portrait photography sessions, or leading teen ministry at her church, where she guides teenagers each Sunday.

Connect with Ronnie and the Third Act Society:

Website: www.ThirdActSociety.com

YouTube: @ThirdActSociety

Community: skool.com/third-act-society

Newsletter: thirdactsociety.substack.com

Instagram: @thirdactsociety

Facebook: Third Act Society

For speaking inquiries: info@thirdactsociety.com

Speaking & Workshops

Bring the Third Act journey to your community

Does your organization serve women navigating life transitions? Are you planning a retreat, conference, or event for mothers facing the identity shift?

Ronnie Izon brings a decade of Third Act living to audiences hungry for hope, humor, and practical wisdom about life after intensive motherhood. Her presentations combine personal storytelling with actionable insights, creating spaces where women feel understood, encouraged, and equipped to embrace their next chapter.

Popular Speaking Topics:

"The Third Act is Calling: Discovering Your Purpose After Motherhood" *Perfect for women's conferences, church retreats, and corporate events*

"From Carpool Driver to Travel Enthusiast: Redefining Freedom in the Third Act" *Ideal for lifestyle and wellness events*

"Faith Through Transition: Spiritual Growth in the Empty Nest" *Designed for faith-based organizations and ministries*

"The Art of Letting Go: Parenting Adult Children with Grace" *Essential for parenting conferences and family-focused events*

"Building Your Third Act Community: Creating Connection in a New Season" *Perfect for networking events and professional development*

Presentation Formats:

- Keynote presentations (45-90 minutes)
- Interactive workshops (2-6 hours)
- Multi-day retreats
- Virtual events and webinars
- Panel discussions and Q&A sessions

What you can expect:

Authentic storytelling from someone still living the transformation, not theorizing from a distance. Ronnie brings a decade of real Third Act experience - the messy, beautiful, ongoing work of reinvention that happens when you choose yourself after intensive motherhood.

You'll leave with:

- Permission to dream beyond your current circumstances
- Practical tools for navigating major life transitions
- A new framework for viewing this season as beginning, not ending
- Connection with other women on similar journeys

Book Ronnie for your next event:

- **Email:** speaking@ThirdActLiving.com
- **Website:** www.ThirdActLiving.com/speaking
- **Phone:** Available upon request

Custom programming available for organizations with specific needs or themes.

Resources for Your Third Act

Resources for Your Third Act Journey

Because transformation requires tools, not just inspiration

Essential Reading for Women In Transition

Books that understand this exact season:

- "Option B" by Sheryl Sandberg - *Resilience after life's unexpected turns*
- "The Gifts of Imperfection" by Brené Brown - *Embracing vulnerability as strength*
- "A New Earth" by Eckhart Tolle - *Spiritual awakening through life transitions*
- "Empty Nest, Full Life" by Cynthia Peckinpaugh - *Practical wisdom for this transition*
- "The Second Half of Life" by Angeles Arrien - *Finding meaning in midlife*

Faith-Based Resources for Transition

When you need spiritual grounding:

- "Falling Upward" by Richard Rohr - *Spirituality for the second half of life*
- "Present Over Perfect" by Shauna Niequist - *Choosing a simpler, more soulful way of living*
- "Jesus Calling" by Sarah Young - *Daily devotional for uncertain seasons*
- **Online:** She Reads Truth app - *Daily Bible reading plans*

- **Podcasts:** "That Sounds Fun" with Annie F. Downs, "The Next Right Thing" with Emily P. Freeman

Solo Travel Resources (From Someone Who's Actually Done It)

Start here if you've never traveled alone:

- **Women-only tours:** Adventure Women, Women Traveling Together
- **Solo travel communities:** Solo Travel Society (Facebook group with 100k+ women)
- **Safety apps:** bSafe, TripWhistle Global SOS
- **Planning:** Rome2Rio (route planning), TripIt (itinerary organization)

Ronnie's personal recommendations:

- **Dubai experiences:** Contact hello@thirdactsociety.com for group trip opportunities
- **Customized culinary & safari adventures:** SelfishMe Travel (selfishmetravel.com) - *Curated experiences for the sophisticated traveler*
- **Solo-friendly destinations:** Ireland (incredibly welcoming), Iceland (safe and stunning), Japan (solo travel paradise)
- **Travel insurance:** World Nomads (comprehensive coverage for adventurous spirits)

Community and Connection

Find your people:

- **Community:** skool.com/third-act-society (deeper discussions and support)

- **Third Act Society:** thirdactsociety.substack.com (our growing community)
- **Local:** Meetup.com (search "empty nest," "women 50+," "solo travel")
- **Facebook Groups:** "Third Act Society" "Empty Nest Moms," "Women Over 50," "Solo Female Travelers Over 40"
- **LinkedIn:** "Midlife Women's Network," "Career Pivot"

Learning and Growth

Feed your curiosity:

- **Free/Low-cost:** Coursera (audit university courses), Khan Academy, local library programs
- **Creative skills:** CreativeLive, Skillshare, YouTube University
- **Master classes:** MasterClass.com (cooking, writing, photography)
- **Local opportunities:** Community colleges (senior audit programs), art centers, photography clubs

Professional Reinvention

If work is part of your Third Act:

- **Skills assessment:** StrengthsFinder 2.0, Myers-Briggs online
- **Career transition:** LinkedIn Learning, SCORE mentors (free business advice)
- **Entrepreneurship:** Small Business Administration (SBA.gov), local SCORE chapters
- **Networking:** Professional women's organizations, industry meetups

Mental Health and Wellness

Support for the emotional journey:

- **Apps:** Headspace (meditation), Calm (sleep and anxiety), Insight Timer (free meditation)
- **Therapy:** Psychology Today (find therapists specializing in life transitions)
- **Support groups:** Find local empty nest support groups through hospitals, churches, community centers
- **Books:** "The Mindful Way Through Depression," "Rising Strong" by Brené Brown

Practical Life Management

Tools for organizing your new life:

- **Goal setting:** Passion Planner, Bullet Journal method
- **Finance:** Mint (budgeting), Personal Capital (investment tracking)
- **Travel planning:** TripAdvisor, Airbnb, Skyscanner
- **Learning:** Duolingo (languages), Lumosity (brain training)

Creative Expression

Rediscover your artistic side:

- **Writing:** 750words.com (daily writing practice), local writing groups
- **Photography:** Improve Photography podcast, local photography meetups
- **Art:** Jerry's Artarama (supplies), local art studios offering classes

Reflection and Planning Tools

Questions to guide your journey:

Weekly Check-ins:

- What brought me joy this week?
- What drained my energy?
- What am I curious about?
- What would I try if I knew I couldn't fail?

Monthly Deep Dive:

- How have I grown since last month?
- What patterns am I noticing in my choices?
- What's calling to me that I'm ignoring?
- How can I honor both who I was and who I'm becoming?

Quarterly Vision Setting:

- If this season had a theme, what would it be?
- What would make this quarter feel successful?
- What support do I need to ask for?
- How do I want to feel at the end of these three months?

Emergency Self-Care Kit

For the hard days (and there will be some):

- **Immediate comfort:** Favorite tea, cozy blanket, playlist that makes you feel strong
- **Phone a friend:** List of three people who understand this journey
- **Movement:** 10-minute YouTube yoga, walk around the block, dance to one song
- **Perspective:** Read one chapter of this book, write three things you're grateful for

- **Professional help:** Therapist's number, crisis hotline: 988 (Suicide & Crisis Lifeline)

Economic Statistics:

- Fortune: "Women are officially the economy's power players - outpacing men in both income and spending growth, BofA report says," Eleanor Pringle, January 22, 2025
- Entrepreneur: "This One Demographic Will Receive 'Most' of the $124 Trillion Great Wealth Transfer," Sherin Shibu, March 12, 2025

Note: The 73 million women and $15 trillion global wealth figures referenced throughout this book are derived from analysis of data presented in these sources.

Remember This

The Third Act isn't about having all the answers. It's about being brave enough to ask new questions and patient enough to let the answers unfold.

Your journey won't look like anyone else's, and that's exactly as it should be.

You're not starting over. You're starting fresh.